Elder Wyatt,

May your journey in life gurantee a smooth entrance into the "True Life" Preparation is everything in this walk. God bless you always,

In Christ's Love,
Sis Yvonne

Thanks Death
You Did Me A Favor

Bishop Clifton Jones

authorHOUSE®

AuthorHouse™
1663 Liberty Drive
Bloomington, IN 47403
www.authorhouse.com
Phone: 1-800-839-8640

First published by AuthorHouse 5/17/2010

ISBN: 978-1-4520-2362-5 (sc)
ISBN: 978-1-4520-2363-2 (hc)

Library of Congress Control Number: 2010906590

Printed in the United States of America
Bloomington, Indiana

This book is printed on acid-free paper.

I DEDICATE THIS BOOK TO: LADY CARAN TURNER:
Your questions on the subject of death provoked me to address
the subject. Thanks for your motivating questions they were
the inspiration, I needed to put this material together.

Table of Contents

- Introduction ix
- Death Shouldn't Be a Surprise 1
- Thanks Death You Did Me a Favor. 7
- Heaven Says Death Is Ok: (In The Lord) 17
- That Day Is Sure to Come. 37
- Satan Is at It Again. 45
- The Attitude a Difference Maker 55
- An Earthly Thing with Spiritual Ramifications 69
- A Sober Look at the Reality of Death 79
- Fixed tor Living with No Plans for Dying 91
- Long Life or Right Living; (Think About It) 105
- A Pre-Death Reviving: (The Need of the Hour) 113
- Living Life to Miss Dying Twice 121
- Death by One, The Resurrection by the Other 133

Introduction

I don't know of a more dreaded subject than that of death. We tend to act as if it should be ignored.

We may not discuss the matter but our failure to talk about it won't prevent it from coming. Death has an invitation to visit every living person some day. It is true that none of us know what day it is set to visit us, but we know it is sure to come.

I think the time to think and to talk about death is now, if we would give serious thought to the subject, that would no doubt aid us in making proper preparation for that day.

It would be tragic to have lived many years on this earth but fail to secure a place in the future. I am sure if we would fail to prepare for a future home it wouldn't be because we didn't know that we had to move.

Many of us have been around long enough to have seen multitudes leave this earth by way of death. We have no doubt had someone that was near and dear to us to depart from this life. With each death, we should have caught the hint that it happens to all, the good, bad and the wicked as well as the righteous. There is no prescribed way to live to prevent death. However, there is a way to live to prevent death from making things worse. If we live in accordance to God's word, He will provide us with a home much better than the one we must leave.

I trust that the material contained in this book will serve as a sober reminder that death is not the problem. It would be the way we lived that will make the difference. If we die in the Lord, we would then be His total responsibility. You could be sure that He knows well how to provide for His own.

Every born again believer has a very bright future, in fact, the outlook for a believer is so much more appealing than this life. We should gladly agree with the scriptures.

- **"And I heard a voice from heaven saying unto me, Write, Blessed are the dead which die in the Lord from henceforth: Yea, saith the Spirit, that they may rest from their labours; and their works do follow them." (Rev 14:13)**

The word of God calls dying in the Lord a blessing. Since it is called a blessing by the Master, who are we to say differently?

I am sure that you know the catch to making death a blessing would be dying in the Lord. That should be the goal of each born again believer. We should strive to live according to the will of God; that will keep us in fellowship with Him. If we maintain a consistent walk with the Lord dying would be a reward to us. It would open the door for us to enter the life that we would have prepared for.

Not only did the word say that it is a blessing to die in the Lord, it said that one would rest from labor. If we would live as we should, I am sure that we would some day grow humanly tired. Dying in the Lord would provide us that much need rest.

Death Shouldn't Be a Surprise

The first family should have been the only ones amazed by death since it commenced with Abel, their son as the first recorded death. Since that time, every living person has seen death come and take away loved ones, friend, enemies, heroes and well wishers. The list is long that contains the name of the deceased and that record is growing everyday.

I can assure you that death may yet be a mystery. It may be at the top of the list when it comes to things we just don't understand. However, it should not come as a surprise, because we have seen it too often to qualify as a surprise.

Just think the earth would be overpopulated if every person that had ever lived were yet alive today. That could be one good human way to view death. However, I am confident that the Lord has a much better reason in mind than the over population of the earth.

The Lord wants man to spend eternity with Him. Since sin contaminated the earth and caused Him to curse it, the Lord's original plan did not call for death. It was ushered in by sin. That is the thing that made it necessary for the Lord to prepare a place where sin could not enter, a much better place than this universe, a place that could not be overpopulated and where sin could not enter in.

The place that the Lord has prepared for His children, these cursed bodies cannot enter. The place that the Lord has prepared is a prepared place for prepared people. That is why one must be born again to enter that eternal resting place that the Lord has prepared for His obedient children.

As painful and sad as death may be to us in this life, in the life to come God's eternal plan is sure to wipe away all tears and sorrow.

Our greatest comfort should rest in the fact the Lord knows how to run His business. He made the earth a wonderful place to dwell, it was sin that disrupted that happy and peaceful place.

After the garden was invaded by sin, the Lord made sure that the next place He prepared for His children, sin could in no wise enter in.

The born again experience would put a soul in right standing with the Lord and equip one with the contents that eternity is made of. It is the new birth that puts us in Christ. We are given His divine nature, that is the thing that makes us suited for eternity with Him.

- **"Therefore if any man be in Christ, he is a new creature: old things are passed away; behold, all things are become new." (2 Cor 5:17 KJV)**
- **"Blessed be the God and Father of our Lord Jesus Christ, who hath blessed us with all spiritual blessings in heavenly places in Christ:**
- **According as he hath chosen us in him before the foundation of the world, that we should be holy and without blame before him in love:" (Eph 1:3-4 KJV)**
- **"According as his divine power hath given unto us all things that pertain unto life and godliness, through**

the knowledge of him that hath called us to glory and virtue:

- **Whereby are given unto us exceeding great and precious promises: that by these ye might be partakers of the divine nature, having escaped the corruption that is in the world through lust." (2 Peter 1:3 KJV)**

The Apostle Peter tells us that we have been given His divine nature. That is the part that never dies, it is the shell that we live in that dies and goes back to the dust. The part that the Lord is truly interested in is that part that contains His divine nature, the part that has been born again. That is the main reason a person has to be born again to avoid making death a sad ending of his or her eternal future.

The born again person is transferred by death to his or her assigned place. He or she is not hurt by death. It is somewhat like eating nuts, the shell is not what we want, and it is the treat on the inside that one would seek. Once the nut is cracked and the goody removed, the shell is no longer important. Likewise, when one dies, it is the divine nature that is important to the Lord. The shell is placed back into the earth and the Lord takes the goody or the soul home with Him to enjoy throughout eternity.

We could say in essence that death is viewed the way it is because of our failure to see the divine role in death. All we seem to see is the sadness it brings. We fail to realize that the Lord is the manager of it all, He wouldn't allow death to put an end to what He knows is best for His children. He has it arranged so that death can only touch the part that has no eternal value. Once death removes the inferior part that it is no longer needed, the soul and its Savior would be forever joined together for all eternity.

Another reason we should not be surprised by death, the Lord has provided us with a wealth of information on the subject. If we believe the word, it would be almost impossible not to know that death is sure to come to all living.

The subject of death is found in both Testaments beginning with the first man, he was told where he would go after his journey ended here on earth. Man was taken from the dust of the earth in the beginning, he would be deposited back into the earth when his life ended.

- **"In the sweat of thy face shalt thou eat bread, till thou return unto the ground; for out of it wast thou taken: for dust thou art, and unto dust shalt thou return." (Gen 3:19 KJV)**

Death is as sure as life. All that are born of a woman must someday die, we have no choice in the matte of death. We didn't choose to be born and we are not the ones that chooses when we die. It is important that we choose how we die. That is, what our spiritual status is when we die, that matter is managed by the way we live daily.

- **"For we must needs die, and are as water spilt on the ground, which cannot be gathered up again; neither doth God respect any person: yet doth he devise means, that his banished be not expelled from him." (2 Sam 14:14 KJV)**
- **"Seeing his days are determined, the number of his months are with thee, thou hast appointed his bounds that he cannot pass;" (Job 14:5 KJV)**
- **"For I know that thou wilt bring me to death, and to the house appointed for all living." (Job 30:23 KJV)**

Anyone reading the word of God is sure to discover the fact that death is the end of the living here on earth. The time we live should be fully used preparing for the hour of death, because it is an appointment that is impossible to break. When the Lord gets ready, we must move to our eternal homes. Ready or not, we must depart from this life.

- **"And as it is appointed unto men once to die, but after this the judgment:" (Heb 9:27 KJV)**
- **"What man is he that liveth, and shall not see death? shall he deliver his soul from the hand of the grave? Selah." (Ps 89:48 KJV)**
- **"All go unto one place; all are of the dust, and all turn to dust again." (Eccl 3:20 KJV)**
- **"For the living know that they shall die: but the dead know not any thing, neither have they any more a reward; for the memory of them is forgotten." (Eccl 9:5 KJV)**

The word of God leaves no doubt that death is sure to come to all living. Since we know it is coming we should be more diligent in our preparation since we can't prevent its coming.

To prevent us from being surprised the Lord has left on record much information on the subject. In order to enhance our knowledge, we have been given time. All living has seen someone die during our short stay here on earth, and if we continue to live, we are sure to see many more depart this life through death.

The departure of everyone we know about, could serve as a reminder that we too must go that way. If we would wisely consider that the dying of others is a refresher course in reality, we would improve our status in preparation for our time.

Thanks Death You Did Me a Favor.

It takes a spiritual eye, mind and heart to visualize death as a favor; however, the word of God supports that concept. It pictures dying as the way to get into the presence of the Lord.

The Apostle Paul said that living in this body constitutes being absent from the Lord and dying would take you into His presence. With that being true, death would be doing a believer a favor.

- **"Therefore we are always confident, knowing that, whilst we are at home in the body, we are absent from the Lord:" (2Cor 5:6 KJV)**

When we weigh in on the above fact, we get a clearer picture as to why these bodies are so frail and so quickly decay. They were not given to us to last forever, but long enough to prepare for our everlasting home.

We should learn to live in these temporary homes knowing that they are exactly transitory, that our lasting home should be ready after this one expires.

Our focus should be centered on moving. Moving is not a problem for the person that makes preparation prior to departing, it only becomes a hardship when one has to move but has no where to go.

We have been informed that the decaying of our earthly home is to be expected, but none of what happens to this old house of clay interferes with the building not made with human hands, that house beyond the sky.

Just as we have lived in this old house of clay, we shall spend eternity in the building not made with hands. The place the Lord prepared for us shall receive us, and we shall abide with Him forever.

- **"For we know that if our earthly house of this tabernacle were dissolved, we have a building of God, an house not made with hands, eternal in the heavens.**
- **For in this we groan, earnestly desiring to be clothed upon with our house which is from heaven:**
- **If so be that being clothed we shall not be found naked.**
- **For we that are in this tabernacle do groan, being burdened: not for that we would be unclothed, but clothed upon, that mortality might be swallowed up of life." (2 Cor 5:1-KJV)**

When death comes to take us out of these crumbling bodies that are often filled with pain, discomforts and heartaches, one could then look up on death as a favor.

The reason we could be able to look upon death as a favor because it is death that removes us from this old house of clay and opens up the way for us to move into our brand new home.

The new house is superior to the one we now dwell in. Our new home has zero flaws and zero ending. The good part is that we will be with Jesus forever.

- **"And God shall wipe away all tears from their eyes; and there shall be no more death, neither sorrow, nor crying, neither shall there be any more pain: for the former things are passed away." (Rev 21:4 KJV)**

We may not comprehend on this side that death is a favor. However, the crossover to the other side would reveal what we had been unable to see on this side. We would quickly discover that dying was a favor, for it removes a saint from the earth into the presence of the Lord.

We have Lazarus, one that suffered greatly in this life, then death did him a favor. It moved him into a resting place in the bosom of Abraham. The transfer healed all of his hurts and solved his problems. That sounds like a real favor to me, what Lazarus received was far better than what he had in this life. By faith, the results of Lazarus would be what all believers would receive after death a final resting place where earthly problems would no longer exist.

As a believer, all we have to go on is the word of God which is enough because every promise is yea and amen. There is nothing on earth more reliable than God's word.

The Apostle Paul was a strong advocate that dying was a blessing, when his time came to give up his life on this side he said that he was ready:

- **"For I am now ready to be offered, and the time of my departure is at hand.**

- **I have fought a good fight, I have finished my course, I have kept the faith:**
- **Henceforth there is laid up for me a crown of righteousness, which the Lord, the righteous judge, shall give me at that day: and not to me only, but unto all them also that love his appearing." (2 Tim 4:6-8 KJV)**

The Apostle Paul sounded like a person that is dressed and ready waiting for his ride. There is absolutely no indication that he dreaded what was about to happen. Is that because he considered death as a favor?

To protect us from feeling that death would serve as a favor to super saints or Bible saints only, the Apostle said that the same blessing would be awaiting all that loved the Lord's appearing. That should include every blood-washed, spirit-filled believer better yet, you and me.

Paul advances the idea that the Lord could be glorified in death as well as in life. We easily recognize the favors of the Lord in this life, but find it very difficult to visualize death as bringing honor to the Lord.

I would like to say that living for the Lord according to His word inspires confidence in the heart. I believe the closer one walks with the Lord, the higher his or her level of confidences rises. That is the reason the Apostle could sound so assured, he had walked the walk, and that made it easy for him to talk the talk.

The reason the Apostle was not intimidated by the threat of death, he was confident that the message he had preached to others was true. He felt that it would work for him as well because he had therefore, walked the walk and talked the talked.

I think the Lord would have every believer to plug into that boldness and courage and make it a part of our daily lives. We should see death as blessing in disguise. It comes to remove us from the face of the earth, but has not power to prevent us from entering the presence of the Lord.

- **"According to my earnest expectation and my hope, that in nothing I shall be ashamed, but that with all boldness, as always, so now also Christ shall be magnified in my body, whether it be by life, or by death." (Phil 1:20 KJV)**

The secret to living is to have things well enough together so that death would magnify the Lord. When we live saved lives, we are in the Lord and even death cannot change that.

A life lived to the glory of God on earth would continue to glorify Him in heaven. Only the enemy of the soul would be a loser, because the saint and the Lord would both have what they wanted.

The Lord would have held up His end of the bargain to keep us from falling and the saint would have reached his destination where he would spend all eternity with his Lord.

- **"For to me to live is Christ, and to die is gain." (Phil 1:21 KJV)**

The Apostle said that living in that is living in this world benefits or extends one's tenure of service but dying would bring gain. The people that we are allowed to serve would surely benefit from our long period of service, but the server and the Lord would benefit even more after death removes us from this earth. We would then forever be with the Lord, our earthly toil would be over.

It is high time that the church caught the vision of the genuine service rendered by God's ministering servants to the congregation. That person's long service would be a blessing to the body. The church should learn to appreciate the ministry the Lord has provided to serve us. The word reveals that they would be better off if they were with Him.

Every day a true servant of God lives, you can be sure that many would benefit from him or her living. The things done by a child of God sometimes goes unnoticed, but their death reminds you how much you benefited from their lives.

We speak of many things as gain, but rarely do we hear one stating that dying would be gaining.

The Apostle said that dying would be gain to him, because he was fully persuaded that his life was in harmony with God's word. He knew that dying in the Lord would place him in good company and that his death would not be permanent, he would rise again.

That is the level of confidence we need to strive for, we should seek to live life with dying in mind. We should understand that that death is one of those enemies that can do us no harm as long as we are in the Lord.

- **"But if I live in the flesh, this is the fruit of my labour: yet what I shall choose I wot not.**
- **For I am in a strait betwixt two, having a desire to depart, and to be with Christ; which is far better:**
- **Nevertheless to abide in the flesh is more needful for you.**
- **And having this confidence, I know that I shall abide and continue with you all for your furtherance and joy of faith;**

- **That your rejoicing may be more abundant in Jesus Christ for me by my coming to you again." (Phil 1:22-26 KJV)**

It is a fact that death could be looked upon as a blessing in disguise. It is not clear to the natural mind the role that death plays, but as we grow spiritually, we are sure to get a glimpse of its duty.

Death is without a doubt one of the most misunderstood events that takes place on the earth. In spite of its long existence it yet remains a great mystery. It just might be that death is so perplexing because it was not a part of God's original plan for man.

The Lord wanted man to live forever, but sin temporarily interrupted that plan by ushering in sin, death, pain and all the other discomforts that God didn't plan for man.

The original plan for man to live forever in the presence of the Lord, death could never take place in this world, sin destroyed that possibility. However, it didn't destroy the Lord's desire for His creature; He personally took on sin and reopened the door of hope for man to be reunited to Him.

- **"Forasmuch then as the children are partakers of flesh and blood, he also himself likewise took part of the same; that through death he might destroy him that had the power of death, that is, the devil;**
- **And deliver them who through fear of death were all their lifetime subject to bondage." (Heb 2:14-15 KJV)**

Our appreciation for what Jesus did for us through death is sure to come up short when we view death from a human perspective. Our human minds could easily fail to recognize death as a blessing to believers, when we fail to see that the death of Jesus took the sting out of death. Jesus transformed the word death into sleep, that means when a believer departs from this life he/she would be sleeping. Surely a sleeping person can be awakened, but not so with a dead person.

- **"Marvel not at this: for the hour is coming, in the which all that are in the graves shall hear his voice," (John 5:28 KJV)**

Our hope in the resurrection, or life after death, was made possible when Jesus tasted death for every person. Jesus knew that death without Him would bring forth the severest form of death, the kind of death that would kill the spirit as well as the body.

It should be the goal of every child of God to avoid any death that would separate him or her from the presence of the Lord. In other words, we should make every effort to position ourselves to hear the voice of the Lord.

I may add that it would be a good practice to seek to hear and know His voice now so that we won't mistake His voice in the end, because there are many voices sounding in the land today. Just as there are many voices, we need to learn His voice.

The scripture states that the ear should hear what the Spirit has to say.

- **"He that hath an ear, let him hear what the Spirit saith unto the churches; To him that overcometh will I give to eat of the tree of life, which is in the midst of the paradise of God." (Rev 2:7 KJV)**
- **"He that hath an ear, let him hear what the Spirit saith unto the churches; He that overcometh shall not be hurt of the second death." (Rev 2:11 KJV)**

- **"If any man have an ear, let him hear." (Rev 13:9 KJV)**

An ear to hear appears important to one's overcoming in life and overcoming the second death. If we should fail to hear, we would miss too much of what is necessary for our continuance in the Lord.

We have Jesus as our supreme example of preparation for things to come. He faced life with boldness and died for us with courage and surrender. He knew what He wanted and was willing to pay the necessary price.

To keep us from having to taste death, He let death feed upon Him. His death delivered us from having to travel across that rough and rocky road.

Every righteous demand was met in the death of Jesus. It is now our responsibility to live our lives to the glory of His name.

- **"But we see Jesus, who was made a little lower than the angels for the suffering of death, crowned with glory and honour; that he by the grace of God should taste death for every man." (Heb 2:9 KJV)**

I feel that it is impossible for death to appeal to the ones that are left behind as it would for the ones that cross over to that peaceful shore. The death of a loved one would leave us grieving and mourning. If the deceased leaves here as a saint, that soul would be forever relieved of his or her daily burden.

If one has enjoyed being with the Lord in this life, it stands to reason that he or she would enjoy Him the more in the life to come, because there would be no more interruptions.

Being with the Lord forever should be the only motivation a child of God would need to keep him/her motivated to live holy lives. When we consider the fact that the Lord paid such an awesome price to make this possible, we should do whatever it would take to go back with Him when He comes for His church.

I pray to God that we would sense the tremendous sacrifice the Lord made to purchase us from the slave-market of sin, and that we would show our appreciation by making preparation to spend eternity with Him.

I feel strongly that the blessing of the Lord's presence would wipe away all of our bad memories. Because the presence of the Lord would surpass each and ever experience we would have encountered on this earth.

Heaven Says Death Is Ok: (In The Lord)

- "And I heard a voice from heaven saying unto me, Write, Blessed are the dead which die in the Lord from henceforth: Yea, saith the Spirit, that they may rest from their labours; and their works do follow them." (Rev 14:13)

The topic says its ok. This is a word that we use frequently when someone says or does something that meets our approval. Heaven is saying that dying in the Lord is ok. In other words, when one dies in the Lord, that person might leave some on earth sad, but it makes heaven happy.

- Ok; "warmly commending acceptance or agreement" Synonyms: approbation, approval, benediction, blessing, favor, okay (Franklin Language Master)

I think the definition says clearly what heaven is saying when it comes to the death of the righteous; heaven stands ready to stamp its approval on such a death.

What more or what greater approval would one need than to get heaven's approbation that death is all right as long as it is in the Lord? With this kind favor, the thing we need to do is to make sure that our living is according to the word of God. When we have that in order dying in the Lord would take care of itself.

It would be wonderful if we would listen to heaven's voice and align our life with heaven's way of preparing. When death arrived, we would be acceptable.

Anything that heaven approves, you could be sure it also gives instructions for preparation. When a person follow heaven's directions on earth; he or she is assured that his or her reservations would be waiting in glory.

Staying in touch with Jesus, the one that made it possible for us to be acceptable, is a must. We need to stay in touch with Him and to call upon Him for directions and instructions on how to live an acceptable life.

When we maintain a healthy relationship with the Author of eternal life, we are sure to have the level of motivation one needs to continue through this evil world with success.

If one should grow weary, he or she would only need to look at the price the Lord paid in order to offer us an eternal home. One should reason that if I am love to that degree, that he/she should put forth his or her best effort to please their loving benefactor.

- **"And I heard a voice from heaven saying unto me, Write, Blessed are the dead which die in the Lord from henceforth: Yea, saith the Spirit, that they may rest from their labours; and their works do follow them." (Rev 14:13 KJV)**

There has been much conversation on the subject of death over the years and much of what we hear makes death sound as if it is the worst thing that could happen to a person. I think that it's high time that we should let the Lord do some talking on the subject. in the above text, I hear the Lord saying that it's alright to die, that is, if your death is in the Lord. One wouldn't have to be a rocket scientist to know that one dying outside the Lord's approval would meet along and sad eternity.

If anyone would knows what's good for us, it would be the Lord. He says that a person dying in the Lord is blessed. We have spent too much time listening to the mindset of this world. Man's thinking has left us feeling that one is better off to continue to live in this world, rather than die and forever be with the Lord. There has to be something wrong with that kind of thinking. There is no way the Lord would prepare a place for us that would be less gratifying than this world with its many problems.

I would be one of the first to admit that this world has many good, pleasurable, delightful and gratifying things to offer. However, none of what the world has to offer is enough to persuade me to believe that our God has less waiting on the other side.

Dying in the Lord is the divine plan. That is why Jesus came to deliver man from the consequences of the fall which is eternal death. Eternal death means that one is cut off from the presence of the living God forever and ever.

The reward of dying in the Lord is the blessing of spending eternity with the Lord. When death comes to a believer, he or she moves from labor to reward.

When we view death from the scriptural stand point, we get altogether a different perspective. The Bible characters seemed to have accepted the fact that death too was one of the stages that one would pass through to get to the other side.

We have been put into a position to give us an even better understanding of death. We have the record of both Testaments. In the Old, we saw that sin was not a part of the original plan, it entered in because of man's disobedience. It was passed to all men.

It is my understanding that the Lord intended that man should never die, when man did disobey the voice and will of God, that is when death entered the human race.

We could correctly say that sin brought in death. That being true, when we have our sins forgiven, that would mean that death is no longer to be feared. The removal of the curse of sin would make us new creatures. The Lord would be able to receive into His everlasting kingdom all that are born again.

The energy we spend worrying about death and the fear we feel when the subject is brought up, could easily be brought under control if we would spend more time focusing on the sin problem. If we would take full advantage of God's salvation plan, we would be ready for death's arrival.

To die with confidence, one would have to live making preparation. To fail in preparing would mean failure in death. According to the teachings of the Bible, no one fails in death that succeeds in preparation.

- **"Then said Martha unto Jesus, Lord, if thou hadst been here, my brother had not died.**
- **But I know, that even now, whatsoever thou wilt ask of God, God will give it thee.**
- **Jesus saith unto her, Thy brother shall rise again.**
- **Martha saith unto him, I know that he shall rise again in the resurrection at the last day.**

- **Jesus said unto her, I am the resurrection, and the life: he that believeth in me, though he were dead, yet shall he live:**
- **And whosoever liveth and believeth in me shall never die. Believest thou this?" (John 11:21-26 KJV)**

Jesus didn't mind sharing with Martha His plan to deal with death. If we believe the teachings of the Master, death would not be a problem. The problem would be the way we choose to live our lives, if we would correct how we live, the Master could take it from there.

Life is not to be lived for personal satisfaction outside of a holy lifestyle. We are to live for Christ, since He died for us. Our lives are not our own, they belong to Him. He purchased the total person. Now the total man belongs to Him, and He expects us to live to the glory and honor of His name.

In my opinion King David expressed one of the clearest views that could be presented after the death of a loved one.

- **"But when David saw that his servants whispered, David perceived that the child was dead: therefore David said unto his servants, Is the child dead? And they said, He is dead.**
- **Then David arose from the earth, and washed, and anointed himself, and changed his apparel, and came into the house of the LORD, and worshipped: then he came to his own house; and when he required, they set bread before him, and he did eat.**
- **Then said his servants unto him, What thing is this that thou hast done? thou didst fast and weep for the child,**

- while it was alive; but when the child was dead, thou didst rise and eat bread.
- And he said, While the child was yet alive, I fasted and wept: for I said, Who can tell whether GOD will be gracious to me, that the child may live?
- But now he is dead, wherefore should I fast? can I bring him back again? I shall go to him, but he shall not return to me." (2 Sam 12:19-23 KJV)

While the child was alive, David spent his time in fasting and prayer but after the child died, he arose, tidied himself, went into the house of the Lord, worshipped, went home and started eating again.

A true child of God would surely find strength to carry on if he or she would honor the Lord in spite of what has happened. We see this same pattern carried out by Job after losing ten children.

I find zero supports in the scripture for behaving any other way. There is no support for weeping and wailing as we carry on. We should do our weeping when our loved ones fail to give their lives to the Lord. We know that failure to live for the Lord would result in the worst form of death. Now that could give us reason for weeping on this side.

When our loved ones leave this life after having made the preparation for the life to come, we should rejoice. They would have made the journey that we must surely make. Now we would be shouldered with the responsibility of maintaining a saved life so that our departure would be divinely approved.

- "While he was yet speaking, there came also another, and said, Thy sons and thy daughters were eating and drinking wine in their eldest brother's house:

- **And, behold, there came a great wind from the wilderness, and smote the four corners of the house, and it fell upon the young men, and they are dead; and I only am escaped alone to tell thee.**
- **Then Job arose, and rent his mantle, and shaved his head, and fell down upon the ground, and worshipped,"(Job 1:18-20 KJV)**

When he was questioned concerning his actions, he revealed a truth that the whole human race needs to recognize. We need to know that once a person leaves this life, he or she won't return again as we have known him or her. The next move would be on the part of the living, there in no need to expect a deceased person to come back to us, but it is certain that we are going to depart from this life just as the deceased has done.

The words spoken by the King after the death of his son, are a tremendous revelation. He got cleaned up and went into the house of God and worshipped. That tells me that after someone dies, it time to return to what you would normally do.

It should make us jealous to see an Old Testament brother with such keen insight. We are yet struggling with the reality of losing loved ones. We sometimes act as if the world has suddenly come to an end. We act as if there will be no tomorrow without that the one that passed on.

In reality, when a person dies there is absolutely nothing the living could do to change what has been done. Since that is the case, a person would be better off if he/she would look at it from the realistic view point. This matter is out of my hands, but the Lord is yet worthy to be praised. I promise you that we would get healed much faster in the presence of the Lord than we would surround by multitudes of mourners.

In our society the loss of a loved one seems to so devastate us to the degree that we have no mind to worship, work or carry out any other responsibility. Some even lose their appetite for days.

I suppose the way we carry on after the loss of a loved one is due to our ignorance, selfishness and unwillingness to own up to the fact that none of us are here to stay. We are just passing through or dwelling here until the Lord chooses to take us out of this life.

It is understandable that the longer we have someone in our lives, the more attached we get the ones we love. When death comes to take away one that is dear to us, we feel the loss. I am sure that our feeling of loss is normal but think, the Lord has left enough information on record to better educate us to the reality of death.

It is a bit naive to overlook the fact that death is a sure as life. The only question would be, when will it come because we should know that it is going to come one day? We should also know that loving a person won't keep them from dying. The only thing loving a person does when he/she dies is placing a heavier spirit upon the ones left behind.

We are told that the book of Job is one of the oldest books in the Bible. That being true; we should notice that it too contains thoughts on the subject of death and dying. The man of God understood that some change had to take place. He sensed that his physical body would be consumed by worms once he was deposited back in the dust.

We can look today upon what Job said with a greater understanding. We understand that our natural bodies are to be deposited back into the earth. We know that based upon what Jesus taught and did that there will be a resurrection. The physical body would return to the dust, but the spirit would rise from the dust to spend eternity apart from the body.

- **"For I know that my redeemer liveth, and that he shall stand at the latter day upon the earth:**

- **And though after my skin worms destroy this body, yet in my flesh shall I see God:**
- **Whom I shall see for myself, and mine eyes shall behold, and not another; though my reins be consumed within me." (Job 19:25-27 KJV)**

Somewhere in the preceding verses, everyone should focus on and embrace a strong confidence that life doesn't end just because one departs this world. If we truly comprehended that, we should be motivated to live with a high expectation of seeing the Lord for ourselves.

We must not let this world and its many delights blind our eyes to the hope that rests in the life to come. We cannot afford to believe that it is better here than it would be in the afterlife. If we should allow that concept to seduce us, it stands to reason that we would spend most of our efforts getting all that this world has to offer. However, if we believed that the life to come never ends and we go from labor to reward, we would then wear this world as a lose garment ready and willing to put it off and leave this world behind at the sound of His voice.

I know that the majority of us spend much more time trying to achieve all that we can in this life. We spend endless amount of energy toiling to get ahead or outshine everyone else with our importance. We seem to forget that once we leave here, none of what we have achieved will follow us into the next life.

Just think, we spend great efforts to succeed, achieve, and obtain. We hustle as if this life is the only one that really counts. However, we know just the opposite is true; the thing that counts most is a person's relationship with his or her Lord. It is impossible to die in the Lord without first getting in Him and maintaining a relationship with Him.

Let me say here, one of the saddest scenarios of today is that many of the senior saints are losing sight on spiritual freshness. Many act as if they have made it already, and they don't have to get deeply involved in the things of the spirit.

They lose their fire and continue to sit as if it is no big deal. I would like to say as a senior saint, I think the closer we get to the end the more we should seek to renew our relationship.

It would be sad to us that are senior saints to have escaped the lust of our youth, worldly allurement and other youthful hazards and end up dying sitting in the pew. I strongly feel that the major threat to senior Christian's would be apathy, indifference, coldness and lack of focus.

I am persuaded that we should be fruitful all the days of our lives. The longer we have been around the better we should know the Lord and the more we would be able to share Him with others.

According to the word of God, we don't stop because the years add up. We just get richer, deeper and a better in our knowledge of the Lord. It is understandable that some of the things we once did our physical strength my hinder from doing them at the same pace, but we shouldn't allow our frailties to put us on hold. When we can't use our physical vigor, we should focus more than on our wisdom. We should share our wealth of knowledge and experience with someone that could put it to work.

- **"The righteous shall flourish like the palm tree: he shall grow like a cedar in Lebanon.**
- **Those that be planted in the house of the LORD shall flourish in the courts of our God.**
- **They shall still bring forth fruit in old age; they shall be fat and flourishing;" (Ps 92:12-14 KJV)**

- "Not every one that saith unto me, Lord, Lord, shall enter into the kingdom of heaven; but he that doeth the will of my Father which is in heaven.

- Many will say to me in that day, Lord, Lord, have we not prophesied in thy name? and in thy name have cast out devils? and in thy name done many wonderful works?

- And then will I profess unto them, I never knew you: depart from me, ye that work iniquity.

- Therefore whosoever heareth these sayings of mine, and doeth them, I will liken him unto a wise man, which built his house upon a rock:

- And the rain descended, and the floods came, and the winds blew, and beat upon that house; and it fell not: for it was founded upon a rock.

- And every one that heareth these sayings of mine, and doeth them not, shall be likened unto a foolish man, which built his house upon the sand:

- And the rain descended, and the floods came, and the winds blew, and beat upon that house; and it fell: and great was the fall of it." (Matt 7:21-27 KJV)

A person that has no relationship with the Lord is sure to be rejected by Him in the end. As the Lord Jesus instructed His disciples on the importance of knowing Him in this life, we expect Him to know us in the life to come.

Jesus shared with His disciples the dangerous possibility of one rendering service in His name without really knowing Him or without having a genuine relationship with Him. Here, I reason within myself, if it was possible for the ones that were hand-picked by the Master to fail in their pursuit, surely it could happen to me.

We definitely should not take a thing for granted, we should strive with everything within us to obtain and maintain a healthy relationship with the living God. Because in the end, after all has been said and done, the only thing that would matter would be to know Him in the pardon of our sins.

Knowing Him and dying in the Lord to me are synonymous in nature because having one's sins forgiven is the way one gets to know Him. It is also the only way one could be qualified to die in the Lord.

We see from the words of Jesus that the rendering of service in His name is no substitute for relationship. We need to know Him above knowing how to perform miracles or other mighty works. We need to know the one that we are working for better than we know the job. The thing that demonstrates our knowledge of Him is our ability to stand after the flood passes over.

If troubles, trials, or the loss of a loved one should devastate you and kill your joy to the degree that you are no longer able to function as that is a sign that you didn't know the Lord as well as you though you did, or as well as it may have appeared.

Life's difficulties come to reveal one's status in the Lord, when we are anchored in Him. We are not easily moved by life's swift transitions. If we should feel that we are being overcome, it is our privilege to call upon the Lord for help because He is our refuge and strength.

Life has no difficulties that are too hard for our God. He stands ready willing and able to transcend our greatest problem. He is truly our refuge and strength, the thing we come up short in is fully met by Him.

Satan has deceived many into believing that one's positions, material possessions, fame and fortune are much better than having a good relationship with the Lord. Let's consider it from another view, wouldn't it be a down right disgrace to have the ability to write a check for thousands of dollars on this side but end up bankrupt in eternity? There is no lasting benefit in being successful in this life because it has an end and especially if we end up poverty stricken in that unending life. It would be something wrong with that picture. Why should we strive to be more successful in a life that must come to an end than we do for an endless life? To make that mistake, we would have followed the wrong information?

The thing we need to keep in mind, in order to die in the Lord, we must live in Him. The daily life we live must be controlled by the Holy Spirit, that is, if we wish to die in the Lord.

The Lord's holiness would not allow Him to claim as His own, people that would not live according to His holy lifestyle.

The Lord will not violate His own word just make Himself look good. He must maintain His righteous integrity. He will not change and neither will He go beyond His word.

The mystery called death should be expected as much as we expect a birth to take place. It should be common knowledge by now that all that are born of flesh and blood are sure to die.

Just as we expect a pregnant woman to give birth to a child, it should be expected that everyone that is living must die.

It stands to reason that the death of Abel had good reason to be a surprise, because it was a new experience. It was the first death to take place. After the death of Abel the reality of death should have commenced. By now every living person should have gotten the message that death is sure to come. It comes when no one expects it, it takes those we were not expecting to lose.

The death of every person was a message within itself. It was saying to the living, you could be next. It was saying set your house in order because I am coming for you one day.

Maybe one of the reasons we view death the way that we do, we have trouble dealing with reality. When it comes to discussing the subject of death, that subject is treated as if it is too sacred to discuss or to horrifying to think about. However, nothing, we do or think would prevent it from coming.

- **"For the living know that they shall die: but the dead know not any thing, neither have they any more a reward; for the memory of them is forgotten." (Eccl 9:5 KJV "All go unto one place; all are of the dust, and all turn to dust again." (Eccl 3:20 KJV)**

The better we understand the reality of death, the easier it would be to deal with the loss of a loved one. A good understanding of the scriptures prepares us to see death from God's point of view. We would no longer see or think that we had been robbed by the Lord, or that He took from us more than we deserve to lose. On the other hand, that He took our precious one too soon, we don't know but the Lord knows best for us, we must learn to trust Him in all things. A good understanding could help us change the thinking pattern and concept that we generally hold and that is, they left us. If we were more enlightened, it would prepare us to say in our hearts and mind, I will be on, I just don't know when, but for sure I am coming. This would be the realistic approach to death.

We would be in order to admit that the enemy has been successful in getting us to place too much stock in the idea that sickness precedes death. The truth of the matter is every living person is sick enough to die any day and at anytime. You don't have to have any known disease in order to die, that is strictly in the Lord's hands. When He says the time is now, there is absolutely nothing anyone could do about it. You don't have to be ready, I mean spiritually or naturally. If it's your time, ready or not you've got to move.

- **"Thou hidest thy face, they are troubled: thou takest away their breath, they die, and return to their dust." (Ps 104:29 KJV)**

I don't think we needed it any clearer than the way the preceding verse gives it, **"thou takest away their breath, they die, and return to their dust."** The text not only tells us what happens when the Lord withholds the next breath, it also tells us where we are deposited after we stop breathing. We are allowed to return to the earth, that is where we came from and that is where this old flesh is placed after the real person departs from it.

Death, we know is the consequences of sin; however, The Lord made it possible that we could die in Him. All who die in Him shall live again. The enemy can't stop it from taking place no matter how hard he tries.

Faith in the Lord Jesus takes the sting out of death, it makes death a form of transportation. Since we cannot enter heaven the way we are physically, we have to be changed either by death or in the rapture. Both death and the rapture are modes of transportation to get the saints out of this world into the world to come.

The Bible fully supports the fact that all living must die. Since we know that we are not here to stay, it seems to me that we should wise up and make better use of our time. We should know by now after seeing as many people depart from this life as we have seen, that it does happen and anyone of us could be next.

- **"For I know that thou wilt bring me to death, and to the house appointed for all living." (Job 30:23 KJV)**
  "In the sweat of thy face shalt thou eat bread, till thou return unto the ground; for out of it wast thou taken:

> for dust thou art, and unto dust shalt thou return." (Gen 3:19 KJV)
> - "Seeing his days are determined, the number of his months are with thee, thou hast appointed his bounds that he cannot pass;" (Job 14:5 KJV)
> - "And as it is appointed unto men once to die, but after this the judgment:" (Heb 9:27 KJV)

In this country death is glamorized to the degree it has made funeral business a very lucrative business. One of the reasons the funeral business thrives so in America, we try to make ourselves look good by spending excess money on unessential things. Such things as flowers, programs and caskets are appealing to us. We seem to forget that they are going in the ground and no one will see it again under normal circumstances.

The fact of the matter is that the deceased knows nothing about the number of flowers, the type of arrangements or wreaths, people in attendance, caliber of the sermon or what quality of food was served at the repast. We do those things for ourselves, it makes us appear to be loving and caring.

When it comes to an American funeral, much of what we do for the deceased is obviously done to satisfy our own consciences because the dead know nothing. Their cares for this world ended when breath left their body.

Great sums of money are sometimes spent in travel. We supposedly do it to show our deep love for relatives that live in other states. Some of us would feel remiss, if we failed to attend a loved ones home going celebration. After all, what would the people think of us if we didn't attend?

It is sad to think that we show more concern for people after they are dead than we do during their life-time.

After a person dies, we feel that person should have the very best, even if it means borrowing money to carry out what we consider to be a good funeral. It is a good chance that we had an opportunity to do something for the person while he or she lived but refused to do so. After the Lord called them home, as we love to use the expression, we then try to make them look good and us by doing elaborate things to impress others and make ourselves look as if we really loved the deceased.

Perhaps we are supposed to put loved ones away nicely. Maybe they should be given the nicest casket, the best suit or dress, on such an occasion they should have the most popular minister to speak over them. Nevertheless, now this there is absolutely nothing we could do to change things for the departed. The way they prepared and where they made their arrangements is exactly where they will go.

It has been my observation that the words spoken over the deceased are oftentimes things that he or she should have heard while he or she was alive.

I have also heard words spoken over the dead describing him or her very differently than the way the deceased person chose to live. During the ceremony, the deceased is spoken of as a genuine saint. However, while that person lived, his or her lifestyle was very contrary to what was said during his or her funeral.

God forbid that we should lie to a person while he or she is alive or lie on a person while he or she lives. Heaven help us not to lie for anyone after he or she is gone. To stand over a person and speak lies would jeopardize our own souls.

There is nothing we can do for a person once the breath leaves his or her body. If we are truly concerned, we should do all that we could while a person is alive.

It would serve us well to develop a Job-like attitude when it comes to dealing with death. Among loved ones, Job had to bury 10 children at one time, but he never called God into question about his loss or charge God. How Job dealt with such a great loss may be beyond human understanding or could it be that he understood something that we need to grasp and that is, we are not here for the long haul, and we are just temporary dwellers.

- **"And, behold, there came a great wind from the wilderness, and smote the four corners of the house, and it fell upon the young men, and they are dead; and I only am escaped alone to tell thee.**
- **Then Job arose, and rent his mantle, and shaved his head, and fell down upon the ground, and worshipped,**
- **And said, Naked came I out of my mother's womb, and naked shall I return thither: the LORD gave, and the LORD hath taken away; blessed be the name of the LORD.**
- **In all this Job sinned not, nor charged God foolishly."(Job 1:19-22 KJV)**

It was Job's worship that protected him from playing the blame game with God. He did what every true believer must do, and he turned to the one that is well qualified to minister to one's every need.

When we find the grace to worship the Lord before, after or doing a crisis, we can be sure that the Lord will protect us from the invading spirits that seek to depress, stress or cause us to murmur against God. That is why the Lord tells us that we should give thanks in all things, it would be impossible for us to complain and give thanks at the same time. We are better protected from the enemy's attacks when we open our mouth unto the Lord and give Him thanks regardless of the circumstances. It is a proven fact that doing it God's way, the enemies' stuff won't work against us. The enemy won't be able to hold us down when we choose to lift Jesus up.

- **"In every thing give thanks: for this is the will of God in Christ Jesus concerning you." (1Thess 5:18 KJV)**

This
START

That Day Is Sure to Come.

I think that it is high time we turn the table on the way we prepare for the future. I think that more effort should put toward the life that lasts the longest, than we do toward this ending life.

To make this happen it would require a shift of our focus and a redirection of our energies to focus on being more spiritual and less worldly. We need to listen more closely to the cry of the spirit than we do the screaming of the flesh.

The only heaven for the flesh is the one that it finds in this world, no doubt. That is why the flesh strives to get all that it can on this side, because the future for the flesh is to return to the dust.

It is understandable that we are saddened by the departure of our loved ones; however, we should have expected death to come and should have prepared for its arrival. We should draw a page from David's book while our loved ones are alive. We should pray and fast for them. After they are gone, we should worship the Lord for His goodness in allowing us to have them for a period of time.

I recall the day my mother passed, I had to preach in Kosciusko, Ms. The pastor of the church that I was scheduled to preach for heard of the passing of my mother and called me to relieve me of my obligation. I told him that I was preparing to come.

I decided to make the journey alone. After I had gone for a few miles down the highway, I said to the Lord thank you Lord for allowing me to have a mother for fifty-one-years, that was all I needed to relieve my spirit.

I feel that it would have been ungrateful of me to focus on my mother's passing more than the fact that I had fifty-one-years to enjoy her presence. We know that there are many people that don't have that testimony.

When you listen to us at the so-called funeral, you would almost think that God was the one that had made a mistake by taking away our precious ones. However, the truth of the matter is the mistake was made when we put our head in the sand and forgot that all living must one day die. We make another mistake when we fail to prepare our minds to expect it to happen in our family, just as it takes the loved ones of others.

We read and talk on many subjects, but when it comes to death we tend to be more silent if not altogether dismiss it from our daily thoughts and conversations. We treat the subject of death as if it is something that would never happen. However, we know by now that failing to discuss it won't prevent it from making its scheduled appearance.

We are guilty of attending funerals, yet failing to get the message that is right before our very eyes. That understanding is just as the deceased has fulfilled his or her appointment, we must some day do the same.

It is irresponsible of us to let such a clear object lesson appear before our eyes, and we yet fail to make the connections. Funeral time should serve as a silent lesson to all in attendance. We should hear loud and clear that this is the end of all living. Our thinking should be provoked to call to remembrance that preparation should precede death. Now is the time and here is the place to get ready before hand!

The church as a whole need to participate in a death awareness program, we need to raise the minds of God's people toward the reality of death. We can't afford to wait until death comes to make preparation, we must do that before death comes calling.

In the world, we are constantly being informed of some sickness or disease epidemic. We call it cancer awareness, heart awareness, and stroke awareness, etc. The reason for these special acts of information is to alert the masses of the danger of these diseases and how one may delay or prevent or deal with them.

We need to inform the church about death, since we know it's going to come. It would be to every man's advantage to make proper preparation before it comes.

It is useless to live in denial or to avoid thinking and talking about it. We need to engage in much discussion with people that study God's word, and they could help us in our preparation.

We should know by now that earth has nothing that could prevent death. We could eat right and get our proper rest, but that won't stop death. There is no doctor or medicine on the market that can prevent death. It is possible to delay it, but nothing can prevent it. Eating right would help us feel better while we are alive, but in the end death is sure come.

I don't think we could possibly over emphasize the subject of death. The more we talk about it, the more aware it would leave us and the more we think about it, the clearer the matter should loom in our minds and spirits. The knowledge we gain on the subject of death should inspire us to do what we could to prepare for the hour of death.

- **"It is better to spend your time at funerals than at festivals. For you are going to die, and it is a good thing to think about it while there is still time. 3 Sorrow is better than laughter, for sadness has a refining influence on us. 4 Yes, a wise man thinks much of death, while the fool thinks only of having a good time now." (Eccl 7:2-4 TLB)**

It is while we live that we should think about dying, we shouldn't just think about it in a casual way. We should think soberly and godly. We should desire that our death would be much better than our earthly life. Because we are sure to stay forever in our next home, we should want to leave here well prepared for our eternal home.

Just as we think of living we should also consider and make preparation for dying. We can be sure that no amount of thinking or preparing would prevent death from coming, but it sure could help us in being ready, when death comes knocking at the door.

Since we can't stop death from running its course, it would be to our eternal advantage to make some serious preparation for its arrival. Our getting ready should have as its objective to secure a good future for our eternal soul. We should strategize to live with dying in the Lord in mind. Keep in mind that earth has nothing that would compensate for the loss of the soul, this is the teaching of our Lord.

- "For what is a man profited, if he shall gain the whole world, and lose his own soul? or what shall a man give in exchange for his soul?" (Matt 16:26 KJV)

Out of the many blessings we have received from the Lord, none of them compares with the value of the soul. It is the part of us that has eternal value. We should strive to see that it spends eternity with its maker.

All believers are to embrace the same truth that Jesus spoke to Mary and Martha, **"Then said Martha unto Jesus, Lord, if thou hadst been here, my brother had not died.**

But I know, that even now, whatsoever thou wilt ask of God, God will give it thee.

Jesus saith unto her, Thy brother shall rise again. Martha saith unto him, I know that he shall rise again in the resurrection at the last day. Jesus said unto her, I am the resurrection, and the life: he that believeth in me, though he were dead, yet shall he live: And whosoever liveth and believeth in me shall never die. Believest thou this?" (John 11:21-26 KJV)

Faith in the living God is the key that makes death work for one's eternal welfare. When one dies believing, there is nothing that could or would hinder that person from seeing the Lord in peace. May I say along with the word, when one dies in the Lord, he or she is blessed. That being true, we should make it our goal to live in a manner that we would have no problem dying in the Lord.

It may be difficult for the mind to comprehend but the spirit knows right well that God is up to something. When we read the word of God, we get the inner witness of what He has in store. He told Mary that death offered a future for seeing the glory of God.

"Jesus said, Take ye away the stone. Martha, the sister of him that was dead, saith unto him, Lord, by this time he stinketh: for he hath been dead four days.

40 Jesus saith unto her, Said I not unto thee, that, if thou wouldest believe, thou shouldest see the glory of God?" (John 11:39-40 KJV)

When a believer lives in faith, death does not destroy his or her hope. It only makes it possible for the person to enter that awaited future. Dying in the Lord opens the door for Him to raise up the soul after it has left the body or after death.

The hope of a child of God is not this world and its riches. The expectation of a saint is the resurrection of the soul. To live without hope in a better life would be a partially lived life, because the hope of the resurrection is the thing that keeps one inspired to keep looking ahead.

"And this is the Father's will which hath sent me, that of all which he hath given me I should lose nothing, but should raise it up again at the last day. And this is the will of him that sent me, that every one which seeth the Son, and believeth on him, may have everlasting life: and I will raise him up at the last day." (John 6:39-40 KJV)

When our faith in the resurrection from the dead is stronger than our desire for simply living in this mundane world, we are sure to be greatly motivated to live holy lives.

May I say that there wouldn't be a resurrection without a death, so then death is a part of the process. It may be the part that is less acceptable, but it is a part. The sooner we realize it and commence to preparing for its arrival, the sooner we would relieve ourselves of many undo worries fears.

Death is an appointment that everyone will surely keep. Ready or not we must keep this date. Since we don't know when it will occur, it would be wise to live daily as if it would take place today.

In order to die in the Lord, it is necessary that one first get in Him and then continue to abide in Him. That is the safe side of life and the guaranteed way not to be left behind after He comes for His church.

42

- "And as it is appointed unto men once to die, but after this the judgment:" (Heb 9:27 KJV)
- "All go unto one place; all are of the dust, and all turn to dust again." (Eccl 3:20 KJV)
- "For the living know that they shall die: but the dead know not any thing, neither have they any more a reward; for the memory of them is forgotten." (Eccl 9:5 KJV)

Satan Is at It Again.

S atan is having the same measure of success with this highly educated and enlightened generation that he had with the ancient world. He was successful in tricking them into spending their time eating, drinking, marrying and giving in marriage until it was too late to recover. We are duplicating that pattern with little or no variation. In fact, some things that didn't exist in that day are open gain for us today.

The Devil has been successful in getting us to carry out practices that he has never done himself. Satan has never used nicotine, drugs, alcohol, and he has never left his family. He has never committed adultery or fornication, he doesn't do pornography, and he never practices hating his own, he supports them fully, his house is never divided it works together for evil.

This is the short list of things that Satan has promoted among the human race that he has never experienced. His reason for pushing these demeaning practices is that he knows they would separate man from the fellowship of God.

There are many acts of wickedness carried out by mankind that Satan is credited with, but the truth of the matter is many of the practices that he is credited with he don't do himself. We even credit the Devil with our frequent absence from church. Let me ask you a question, when was the last time the devil missed a church service or was late? It would be to our advantage if he stayed home as often as some of the saints do.

Don't get me wrong, I know that the Devil is a promoter of evil, but he is not necessarily the one that carries it out. He makes his suggestions to us and expects us to do what he hasn't done.

The first generation's example should have served as a warning to us. Furthermore, we could have profited from the warning given by the Lord to His followers, **"Watch out! Don't let my sudden coming catch you unawares; don't let me find you living in careless ease, carousing and drinking, and occupied with the problems of this life, like all the rest of the world."(Luke 21:34 TLB)**

Jesus saw what men did in Noah's day. He saw how they placed more emphasis on playing than they did on preparing to escape the flood. Their failure to make preparation was an indication that they didn't believe the message the Lord sent through Noah.

Thank God that Noah left a good example. He was too busy carrying out the will of God to play while the majority was too busy playing to get involved with the work of God. They were much like my generation. Today's world is so busy playing that they don't seem to have time to think of dying. Mankind as a whole is having trouble believing that the coming of the Lord is near. The majority seems to think that time is on their side.

Our God in His wisdom doesn't burden us with the knowledge of the time of death. He reserves that right to Himself. He is the only one that knows when death would come to anyone. However, we don't need to worry about the "when" of death, what we need is to focus on the "how" of death.

Then "when" of death deals with the time of death and the "how" takes in our status at the time of death, we are responsible for how we die, but not when we die.

- **The law of the LORD is perfect, reviving the soul.**
- **The statutes of the LORD are trustworthy, making wise the simple.**
- **The statutes of the LORD are trustworthy, making wise the simple.**
- **The precepts of the LORD are right, giving joy to the heart.**
- **The commands of the LORD are radiant, giving light to the eyes.**
- **The fear of the LORD is pure, enduring forever.**
- **The ordinances of the LORD are sure and altogether righteous.**
- **They are more precious than gold, than much pure gold;**
- **they are sweeter than honey, than honey from the comb.**
- **By them is your servant warned; in keeping them there is great reward." (Ps 19:7-11)(from NIV)**

It is our God given duty to stay in touch with the Master and seek His daily help in keep all known sin from operating in our daily lives. This assignment is without a doubt beyond our human ability but with the Lord's help, it shall be done.

Living right in a wrong world is our responsibility. However, we know we need the Lord's help to succeed in our duty. It is a small thing for Him to aid us; because He has years of experience in assisting His people through difficult tasks. When we trust and obey the rest would be up to Him.

We should not want death to find us under the control of Revelation chapter twenty-one and 8. Because such practices carry a sad ending, we are looking forward to dying in the Lord which opens the door to spend eternity with the blessed.

- **"But the fearful, and unbelieving, and the abominable, and murderers, and whoremongers, and sorcerers, and idolaters, and all liars, shall have their part in the lake which burneth with fire and brimstone: which is the second death." (Rev 21:8 KJV)**
- **"Know ye not that the unrighteous shall not inherit the kingdom of God? Be not deceived: neither fornicators, nor idolaters, nor adulterers, nor effeminate, nor abusers of themselves with mankind,**
- **Nor thieves, nor covetous, nor drunkards, nor revilers, nor extortioners, shall inherit the kingdom of God." (1 Cor 6:9-10KJV)**

We shouldn't want to live under the control of the flesh, because it too is known to be contrary to the will of God. Human nature is known to take sides with the world and the devil. That is why we need to keep the flesh under control lest we lose our soul.

The flesh dreads the thought of dying, because it has been exposed to so many things in this world that it delights in. The flesh is aware that it has no reservations for heaven. Its best days must be enjoyed here on earth. When we fail to discipline the flesh, it is known to run wild because wildness is in all flesh. All is needed is a chance for expression and flesh would commit some serious blunders. The sad side of fleshly gratification is indulgence with sinful connotations, and the spirit must pay the bill. The cost could take an eternity to fully pay.

One of my sayings concerning the flesh, "One should keep a bell and a short lease on the flesh, that way he or she would know at all times where flesh is." To lose sight on the whereabouts of the flesh could mean serious trouble the kind of pains that carry eternal consequences.

- **"Now the works of the flesh are manifest, which are these; Adultery, fornication, uncleanness, lasciviousness,**
- **Idolatry, witchcraft, hatred, variance, emulations, wrath, strife, seditions, heresies,**
- **Envyings, murders, drunkenness, revellings, and such like: of the which I tell you before, as I have also told you in time past, that they which do such things shall not inherit the kingdom of God." (Gal 5:19-21 KJV)**

There are other practices that we shouldn't allow to have an active role in our lives when death calls us home. However, the above list or fleshly activities should suggest to us that we really need the Lord's help in order to be ready for the hour of death.

The wise man Solomon said, *"Yes, a wise man thinks much of death."* The fool thinks just the opposite. He or she is more concerned about having a good time in this present world.

The daily dying of a believer would be the fulfillment of the life of discipline Jesus taught His disciples. Every time we refuse the demands of the flesh, we are dying; this act must be repeated as often as necessary because the flesh is sure to seek gratification as long as it lives.

As long as we walk in the spirit, we are sure to avoid the demands of the flesh and at the same time drive a dagger it to its control. Every measure we take to control the activities of the flesh is doing our spirit a great favor. We would be supporting a bright eternal future.

The thing that made the saints of old so successful is that they were willing to die daily to the things of this world. Moses was willing to forsake Egypt's pleasures because he had hopes that extended beyond the grave.

"By faith Moses, when he was come to years, refused to be called the son of Pharaoh's daughter; Choosing rather to suffer affliction with the people of God, than to enjoy the pleasures of sin for a season; Esteeming the reproach of Christ greater riches than the treasures in Egypt: for he had respect unto the recompence of the reward." (Heb 11:24-26 KJV)

Paul openly counted his earthly successes as dung in order to gain a greater insight and stronger relationship with his risen Lord. He was not impressed with his earthly achievements. Paul was carried away with a desire to better know his Master.

- **"But what things were gain to me, those I counted loss for Christ.**
- **Yea doubtless, and I count all things but loss for the excellency of the knowledge of Christ Jesus my Lord: for whom I have suffered the loss of all things, and do count them but dung, that I may win Christ,**
- **And be found in him, not having mine own righteousness, which is of the law, but that which is through the faith of Christ, the righteousness which is of God by faith:" (Phil 3:7-9 KJV)**

To solidify death we must practice dying daily, the life we live in this world must be marked with daily denials of fleshly aspirations. We must treat the flesh as the servant of the spirit and not the supervisor of boss. We are told by the word of God what our end results would be if we should live after the flesh.

- **"For if ye live after the flesh, ye shall die: but if ye through the Spirit do mortify the deeds of the body, ye shall live." (Rom 8:13 KJV)**

The form of death that is spoken of in the above text is not the kind of death that allows for a resurrection, it is the kind that separates one from the presence of the Lord.

Living after the flesh is just the opposite of dying daily. If we feed the flesh, the spirit is sure to die. However, when feed the spirit would bring death to the flesh.

Dying daily is the lifestyle of believers because our spirit is from above and our bodies are of this world, the spirit will not give in without a fight and the flesh won't give up without one.

The Lord left us enough information to educate our spirits, bodies, and minds that we must disregard the flesh in order to maintain a healthy spiritual position. We must let the flesh die while the spirit continues to move closer to its heavenly home.

- **"As it is written, For thy sake we are killed all the day long; we are accounted as sheep for the slaughter." (Rom 8:36 KJV)**
- **"For I think that God hath set forth us the apostles last, as it were appointed to death: for we are made a spectacle unto the world, and to angels, and to men.**

- We are fools for Christ's sake, but ye are wise in Christ; we are weak, but ye are strong; ye are honourable, but we are despised.
- Even unto this present hour we both hunger, and thirst, and are naked, and are buffeted, and have no certain dwellingplace;
- And labour, working with our own hands: being reviled, we bless; being persecuted, we suffer it:
- Being defamed, we intreat: we are made as the filth of the world, and are the offscouring of all things unto this day." (1 Cor 4:9-13 KJV)
- "Always bearing about in the body the dying of the Lord Jesus, that the life also of Jesus might be made manifest in our body.
- For we which live are alway delivered unto death for Jesus' sake, that the life also of Jesus might be made manifest in our mortal flesh." (2 Cor 4:10-11 KJV)
- "Are they ministers of Christ? (I speak as a fool) I am more; in labours more abundant, in stripes above measure, in prisons more frequent, in deaths oft." (2 Cor 11:23 KJV)

The Devil uses the things of this world as bait to inflame lustful desires in the hearts of the unwatchful and spiritually weak souls. The enemy wants us to get so deeply engaged with having fun that we forget the lateness of the hour or decide that the Lord has changed His mind about coming for the church.

Jesus sited that the day of His coming would be much like the days of Noah and Lot. Based upon that predicament, we should all be looking for His coming by now because our generation is wide open in the practices that He said would take place.

- **They did eat, they drank, they married wives, they were given in marriage, until the day that Noe entered into the ark, and the flood came, and destroyed them all.**
- **Likewise also as it was in the days of Lot; they did eat, they drank, they bought, they sold, they planted, they builded;**
- **But the same day that Lot went out of Sodom it rained fire and brimstone from heaven, and destroyed them all.**
- **Even thus shall it be in the day when the Son of man is revealed.**
- **In that day, he which shall be upon the housetop, and his stuff in the house, let him not come down to take it away: and he that is in the field, let him likewise not return back.**
- **Remember Lot's wife." (Luke 17:26-32 KJV)**

When we consider the message that Jesus was discussing, He was dealing with the danger of not being ready. His direct words to remember Lot's wife should grip the hearts of every believer.

We should be touched because He is talking about His return for His believing children, He points out that Lot's wife's actions should serve as a sober reminder to us that one could lose out on going forward by looking back.

I am struck with the feeling that Lot's wife had too much that she didn't want to leave behind. Her possessions were a great part of her life, so much so that she had to take a last look. That last look proved to be fatal, she turned to a pillar of salt.

I must commend Lot for not allowing the behavior of his wife to overshadow him too. We have no record of Lot turning back to get his pillar of salt. Lot did what we all need to do, he went for himself, and he evidently understood that a person has to decide for him or her. His wife chose to look back.

No matter how much we love a person, we cannot decide for him or her when it comes to walking with the Lord and we shouldn't allow other's wrong decisions to turn us aside from following Him.

There are two important things I know we cannot do for others. Number one, we cannot live for them, and we cannot die for them. Since we cannot live for them, the best thing we could do for them is to show them how life should be lived and keep in mind that our love for them will not prevent them from dying. If the loved one dies in the Lord, we have not lost him or her, he or she would have gone ahead.

Just as Lot's wife looked back against direct instructions, every one of us is subject to do the same thing. We could have so much of what this world offers that we would be busy enjoying it and take our eyes of the coming of the Lord.

The pulpits spent numerous hours charging us with the mindset that the Lord wanted us to prosper in this world. They forgot to tell us that He wanted our souls to prosper too.

Many have died with big homes, fine cars, jewelry, socks and bonds etc. but in their eternal destiny, they would be paupers if they don't know the Lord of glory.

The Attitude a Difference Maker

It is a fact that a person's attitude has much to do with how well he or she survives a crisis, if one should take the wrong approach, there is a good chance the prevailing condition might swallow him/her up.

There is one thing every child of God needs to realize and that is the Lord is in control, even if when doesn't appear that He is. If we would look to Him and ask for His strength to carry on, we would be much better off.

The saints of old seemed to have had an attitude that death was more of a favor than a terror. They would face life's difficulties with courage and boldness. They didn't seek the easy way out of trouble. They met it head on with great expectancy. They knew their God would be with them no matter what happened to their bodies.

When their lives were threatened, they did not count their lives dear unto themselves. They were willing to trust the divine plan, and they were unwilling to accept any easy substitute.

- "Women received their dead raised to life again: and others were tortured, not accepting deliverance; that they might obtain a better resurrection:
- And others had trial of cruel mockings and scourgings, yea, moreover of bonds and imprisonment:
- They were stoned, they were sawn asunder, were tempted, were slain with the sword: they wandered about in sheepskins and goatskins; being destitute, afflicted, tormented;
- (Of whom the world was not worthy:) they wandered in deserts, and in mountains, and in dens and caves of the earth.
- And these all, having obtained a good report through faith, received not the promise:
- God having provided some better thing for us, that they without us should not be made perfect." (Heb 11:35-40 KJV)

It appeared that these dear saints were offered an easier way, but they refused it in the light of eternity. They knew that the Lord had a better offer for their lives, they didn't view this life as the best offer, and their investment had been placed on the life to come.

To benefit from the life to come, we cannot sympathize with the flesh and accept the offers of the world. We must endure the punishment the world inflicts on us and yet maintain our focus on the life to come.

I think the way we view death has much to do with how we live our lives. If we feel that our outcome is God's concern, we live careless, but when we understand that we are responsible for our future after death, we tend to be more conscientious.

The spirit of Thanksgiving is by far the way to go, in fact, the Lord expects His children to give thanks at all times, and this is His will for the lives of believers.

- **"In every thing give thanks: for this is the will of God in Christ Jesus concerning you." (1 Thess 5:18 KJV)**

It is impossible to give thanks and complain and murmur at the same time. As we give thanks, it generates a spirit of gratitude in the hearts. When we start counting our blessings, we are sure to find that we have so much to be thankful for that we don't have time to complain.

Thanksgiving is somewhat like a hard hat, the hat won't keep objects from falling on you but it sure would protect your skull. Likewise, offering thanksgiving won't stop trouble from coming but it sure would protect our spirits from murmuring and complaining.

The Lord is high on His people offing unto Him thanksgiving and praise because that is His way of protecting His children from internal and external destruction.

The very next time you are tempted to complain, disregard that feeling and obey the word of the Lord and offer unto Him thanksgiving and praise and experience the difference in your outlook and feeling.

The Lord knows what's best for us, He wouldn't tell us to do what He was unwilling to assist us in doing. He tells us to offer unto Him thanksgiving knowing what it would do for us as well as how it honors Him.

- **"Whoso offereth praise glorifieth me: and to him that ordereth his conversation aright will I shew the salvation of God." (Ps 50:23 KJV)**

- **"And now shall mine head be lifted up above mine enemies round about me: therefore will I offer in his tabernacle sacrifices of joy; I will sing, yea, I will sing praises unto the LORD." (Ps 27:6 KJV)**
- **"But ye are a chosen generation, a royal priesthood, an holy nation, a peculiar people; that ye should shew forth the praises of him who hath called you out of darkness into his marvellous light:" (1 Peter 2:9 KJV)**

I would like to say when we offer unto the Lord Thanksgiving and praise. We would be fulfilling our duty exactly the way we were created to do. We would be honoring the Lord that made us for the purpose and in the manner. We were made to carry it out.

You know as well as I do that using a thing for its original purpose is the right thing to do. It is not wise to try and run a car in the river it serves best when it is used on the highway. However, a boat would be just right for the river.

Praise is just right for the redeemed, when we offer the Lord praise at all times we are sure to receive His protection from what the enemy would like to convert us into. The Devil would like to hear us complaining at all times. He is a thief and he is out to steal that which matters the most, he would like to steal the praise that belongs to the Lord.

We should know by now that everything that comes our way will not be pleasant to the flesh, but nothing that comes has a right to rob God of the praise that He so rightfully deserves.

I believe a person offering thanksgiving and praise while yet experiencing an extreme degree of trouble, would bring great honor to the faithfulness of the Lord. It would serve as an advertisement that there is of a truth a secret place where one is protected as he or she abides.

- "He that dwelleth in the secret place of the most High shall abide under the shadow of the Almighty.
- I will say of the LORD, He is my refuge and my fortress: my God; in him will I trust.
- Surely he shall deliver thee from the snare of the fowler, and from the noisome pestilence.
- He shall cover thee with his feathers, and under his wings shalt thou trust: his truth shall be thy shield and buckler.
- Thou shalt not be afraid for the terror by night; nor for the arrow that flieth by day;
- Nor for the pestilence that walketh in darkness; nor for the destruction that wasteth at noonday.
- A thousand shall fall at thy side, and ten thousand at thy right hand; but it shall not come nigh thee." (Ps 91:1-7 KJV)
- "Giving thanks always for all things unto God and the Father in the name of our Lord Jesus Christ;" (Eph 5:20 KJV)

That secret place of divine protection is not known by every professor of Christianity, it is reserved for those that seek His face. The thing that makes it a secret place, the majority hasn't found it yet, but once it is found, it is the safest place in the whole wide world.

Offering thanksgiving during a crisis is a true sign that a person has found that place of protection and provision, the place where the Lord rules and His praises are heard.

- "In every thing give thanks: for this is the will of God in Christ Jesus concerning you." (1 Thess 5:18 KJV)

I would like to add, when it comes to giving thanks, the Lord didn't say all things except the death of a loved one, He said all things and always. We must increase our practice of giving thanks, since we must do it in everything and always.

I am fully persuaded that it is the Lord will that we should offer unto Him thanks giving regardless to the circumstances and that would include when death comes to take someone we dearly love.

The command to give thanks in everything and always was issued by the Lord. We fail to understand that when a person dies in the Lord, that person leaves us, but they go to Him. The Lord and that saint is forever united. We make so much unnecessary noise when they leave us because we are denied the person's presence. When they are saved the Lord gladly receives the person, but we feel that we have been robbed.

We have biblical examples of the method of thanksgiving and praise being carried out. That is exactly what David did when he learned that his son was dead, he turned to worship. He took his burden to the Lord and left it there. He did the things that all believers should do, he spent quality time seeking the Lord during the lifetime of the child. When the child died it was time to move on and moving on meant having his spirit refreshed. There is no place of refreshing like the presence of the Lord.

- **"But when David saw that his servants whispered, David perceived that the child was dead: therefore David said unto his servants, Is the child dead? And they said, He is dead.**
- **Then David arose from the earth, and washed, and anointed himself, and changed his apparel, and came into the house of the LORD, and worshipped: then he came to his own house; and when he required, they set bread before him, and he did eat.**

When Job learned that his children were dead, he found his security in the presence of the Lord. He turned to what he had done in the past. Since Job was a worshiper before his children died, he wouldn't let their demise block him from doing what benefited him the most and that was worshiping the Lord.

- **"Then Job arose, and rent his mantle, and shaved his head, and fell down upon the ground, and worshipped,**

The Lord yet deserves our praise regardless to what happens, there is no scriptural support that death is the exception to the rule. The Lord is deserving of our praise, and we shouldn't allow something that we were not prepared for prevent us from offering unto Him thanksgiving.

Those of us that have lost loved ones should do everything within our power to warn them to make preparation for the hour of death. If they refuse to do so, there is nothing we could do to change their status after they depart from this life. Remember the tears we shed, the screaming, the kicking and fainting we do, that's for us not the deceased. None of that helps the departed at all.

We should employ our strongest crying, pleading, begging while people are alive, because there is not a cry that could be made or a tear shed that would alter the person's condition.

I think that the following scriptures present a strong argument that we are obligated to thank and praise the Lord no matter what is taking place in our lives?

- **"I will bless the LORD at all times: his praise shall continually be in my mouth."(Ps 34:1 KJV)**
- **"Let my mouth be filled with thy praise and with thy honour all the day."(Ps 71:8 KJV)**

- "But I will hope continually, and will yet praise thee more and more.
- My mouth shall shew forth thy righteousness and thy salvation all the day; for I know not the numbers thereof." (Ps 71:14-15 KJV)
- "I will extol thee, my God, O king; and I will bless thy name for ever and ever.
- Every day will I bless thee; and I will praise thy name for ever and ever." (Ps 145:1-2 KJV)
- "And my tongue shall speak of thy righteousness and of thy praise all the day long." (Ps 35:28 KJV)
- "I will praise thee, O Lord my God, with all my heart: and I will glorify thy name for evermore.
- For great is thy mercy toward me: and thou hast delivered my soul from the lowest hell." (Ps 86:12-13 KJV)

When we live with the understanding that these bodies are not our own, but they are a loan from the Lord, this kind of knowledge inspires us to treat these bodies differently. The majority of us tend to take better care of borrowed property than we do our own. We seek to return the things we borrow in the best of conditions.

That is exactly the attitude we should have toward these borrowed bodies, we should want to return them holy and acceptable in the sight of the Lord.

Satan knows that praise ushers in the presence of the Lord. That is why he wants us to keep quiet, he knows where the Spirit of the Lord is there is liberty. Where the Spirit of the Lord manifests itself, the supernatural takes place. That is the thing that destroys the yoke of the enemy.

Satan knows that a person under the influence of the supernatural is not likely to take part is his lies and he or she sure won't stop praising the Lord's name.

I truly believe that the Devil delights in our ignorance concerning death because it gives him something to work with and he knows what would work. Our fear of the unknown leaves us vulnerable to his lies and threats.

To prevent us from offering thanksgiving and praise to the Lord, the enemy often uses intimidation tactics. He frequently uses the fear of death to break our spirits. The use of the fear of death is one of the enemy's oldest tricks; however, it yet works on the majority of us. The Devil would have us believe that he could kill us at will. I would rather believe that he would have to get permission before he could carry out his death threat.

Let us reason, if Satan could kill us at will don't you think he would rather do it while we were yet in our sins? The Devil knows that killing a saint wouldn't benefit him at all. Now since it wouldn't benefit him to kill a believer. Why would he want us dead? He really wants to take away our boldness and kill our faith because bold people generate too much enthusiasm for the Lord and the devil can't stand it.

It would be more to the enemy's liking if we would drain in our relationship with the Lord before he strikes. That would benefit him the most, he would have gained another company keep and misery loves company, I am told.

If the enemy should kill us while we are in the Lord the advantage goes to the believer, the enemy could no longer touch when we die in the Lord because we would go, where he could no longer enter.

The next time the Devil threatens you with death, you tell him that he would be doing you a favor if he was allowed to kill you. Once you got rid of him, your troubles would be all over for good.

I am fully persuaded that the things that the Lord has in store on the other side for them that love Him, would far surpass anything we have here in this complex world. I cannot conceive this life having the potential to offer anything that would come anywhere near what the Lord had prepared for us in glory.

One's attitude has much to do with how well or poorly a person deals with life's problems and especially with death. When we take the attitude of gratitude for the life of a deceased person, we deal much better with his or her departure. However, when we view it as a great loss or feel that he or she should have remained with us, we grieve too much and fail to give the Lord due respect for the person's life.

We saw that none of the Bible characters played the blame game with God, they rather bowed down and worshiped the Lord. When we see death from the realistic vantage point I promise you our attitudes would be different.

It is a scriptural fact that a person that is saved would be better off departing this life. We might want to hold on to the departed longer but it is not our call to make that is the Lord's department. Our job is to learn to give thanks in all things and let the Lord do what He does best, that is run this universe His way.

Let me say here, if we continue mourning, weeping and talking about our loss and sadness after one of our loved ones goes home, we are complaining against the Lord. If the Lord had seen fit for the person to remain, nothing would have taken him/her away. The Lord is the only one that can give permission for one to leave this earth, so let us be careful not to cross the line with our grieving. We should adapt the Job like attitude, **"And said, Naked came I out of my mother's womb, and naked shall I return thither: the LORD gave, and the LORD hath taken away; blessed be the name of the LORD.**

In all this Job sinned not, nor charged God foolishly." (Job 1:21-22 KJV)

The same enemy that hates the Lord hates us. He would like to side track us by offering us treasures down here to keep us from spend eternity with our Lord. He would like to see us so busy pursuing the things of this life, that we would forget that heaven is waiting for us.

Jesus warned us not to lay up our treasures here on earth because they would be subject to thieves and robbers.

- "Lay not up for yourselves treasures upon earth, where moth and rust doth corrupt, and where thieves break through and steal:
- But lay up for yourselves treasures in heaven, where neither moth nor rust doth corrupt, and where thieves do not break through nor steal:" (Matt 6:19-20 KJV)

Now if it was possible to take the worries and troubles of this life to the other side that would make the other life just like this one. I am sure that we won't have such concerns plaguing us after this life is over. That is, if we die in the Lord, our cares would all be over.

The Apostle said it best when commented on our hope through the resurrection, he expressed the sadness it would be if our hope ended with this life.

- "If in this life only we have hope in Christ, we are of all men most miserable." (1 Cor 15:19 KJV)

If the Devil had his way, he would keep us too afraid to walk consistently before the Lord. The Devil would like to see us afraid to trust the promises of God. The enemy wants us to feel that the best things in life are right here in this world.

The enemy wants to see us more pleased with the things of the world than we are with going to glory. That is why we need to keep looking into the word of God so that we can keep our priorities straight.

When we read the word of God, we find out what happened to people that put self and things first. We should see their end and choose not to be like them.

The message that was delivered to the rich man in hell could serve as a warning to all on this side, if only we would heed this message.

- **"And he cried and said, Father Abraham, have mercy on me, and send Lazarus, that he may dip the tip of his finger in water, and cool my tongue; for I am tormented in this flame.**
- **But Abraham said, Son, remember that thou in thy lifetime receivedst thy good things, and likewise Lazarus evil things: but now he is comforted, and thou art tormented." (Luke 16:24-25 KJV)**

So called success has blocked the views of many when it comes to the things that are most important. The things we generally go after in this life have no redeeming value, in the afterlife.

The rich man in the above text was very successful in this world. He had so to speak, the finest of everything that his heart could wish but when died none of the things he had obtained mattered anymore. We would be wise to take note of earthly rich heritage versus his poverty stricken end.

Abraham in the text delivered to the rich man the same news that would apply to anyone that would put this enjoyment of this present world ahead of eternal things.

When we choose to enjoy life, in its fullness here, we are sure to come up short in the next life. The rich man made the mistake that many have made and are yet making. That is, living is choosing the good things of life rather than eternal life.

I admit that this world has much to gratify the flesh and entertain the mind but it all ends with this life, and the sad part of it all is in the life to come one would have to pay in eternity for the debt made by his or her fleshly while he/she dwelt on the earth.

That is exactly what Abraham was telling the rich man, he was telling him that he had enjoyed his last good times. He made his choice while he has dwelt on earth, and it was the pay day from that point on.

Jesus *told* us that we would have to deny self in order to follow him. If we are unwilling to say no to our fleshly appetites, we are sure to be lead astray, that would disqualify us from dying in the Lord.

- **"Then said Jesus unto his disciples, If any man will come after me, let him deny himself, and take up his cross, and follow me." (Matt 16:24 KJV)**

An Earthly Thing with Spiritual Ramifications

S atan would rather see us chasing after riches, popularity and fame than to see us pursuing a happy relationship with a person down here on this earth.

The Devil has lied and deceived many out of what could have been a successful marriage. He tricked such minds into believing that it was more advantageous to pursue their own selfish ambitions and lustful desires while neglecting their vowed partner.

Many a person has shipwrecked his or her marriage by getting involved with someone other than his or her mate. At the time, Satan made them feel that the grass was greener on the other side, but once they crossed over they miserably discovered that the difference was just in appearance.

I have said repeatedly that the Devil hates happy people. This seems to be especially true when it comes to marital relationships. Every happy marriage carries with it God's wisdom of relationship, pleasure, joy, peace and commitment.

There is a good chance that true happiness here on earth could serve as a reminder to the Devil of how it was when he was in heaven and how it would be for those accounted worthy to enter that holy city.

- **"Whoso findeth a wife findeth a good thing, and obtaineth favour of the LORD." (Prov 18:22 KJV)**
- **"Live joyfully with the wife whom thou lovest all the days of the life of thy vanity, which he hath given thee under the sun, all the days of thy vanity: for that is thy portion in this life, and in thy labour which thou takest under the sun." (Eccl 9:9 KJV)**
- **"Let thy fountain be blessed: and rejoice with the wife of thy youth.**
- **19 Let her be as the loving hind and pleasant roe; let her breasts satisfy thee at all times; and be thou ravished always with her love." (Prov 5:18-19)**
- It has been my observation that anything that is good for us and honors our God at the same time is heavily targeted by the enemy. That is why it is so common for him declare all out war on every marriage that seeks to come up to divine specification.

The Devil, first of all, hates happy people and specially hates happy homes. He has been in the home wrecking business ever since he talked Adam and Eve out of their happy home. His success over the years has made him a specialist at breaking up homes and making lives miserable.

If you, My Dear Readers, are happily married, he would like to see your marriage on the rocks, but you have some say in that matter, you could call upon your helper and don't stop calling until your deliverance comes.

Too often we see one mate get weak and the other one join him or her. What you should do is seek to strengthen yourself in the Lord and fight for what's yours, getting weak would support the enemies plan to destroy your marriage.

When both partners get spiritually weak, Satan could then move to the next house on his list because the weak ones would destroy one another.

The Lord spoke to us through the wisest ordinary man that ever lived; I am speaking of King Solomon. He had a word for us on the subject of marriage, and I think he knew what he was talking about. He didn't want us to shift our focus too much on things that were not designed to produce the measure of happiness that the Lord wanted us to have.

The Lord wanted us to discover the power of relationship, He wanted it to commence in the home and spread from there. It is a fact that happy homes lead to happy communities and happy neighborhoods results into happy congregations. That is why the enemy is out to put a stop to happiness.

- **"Live happily with the woman you love through the fleeting days of life, for the wife God gives you is your best reward down here for all your earthly toil. " (Eccl 9:9 TLB)**
- **"Let thy fountain be blessed: and rejoice with the wife of thy youth.**
- **19 Let her be as the loving hind and pleasant roe; let her breasts satisfy thee at all times; and be thou ravished always with her love." (Prov 5:18-19 KJV)**
- **"Whoso findeth a wife findeth a good thing, and obtaineth favour of the LORD." (Prov 18:22 KJV)**

- **"House and riches are the inheritance of fathers and a prudent wife is from the LORD"(Prov 19:14 KJV)**

It would be to our advantage to keep our focus clear on what is most rewarding, it appears that marital relationship carries the strongest value of all the things we are allowed to do on this side.

The word of God speaks clearly that a man that finds a wife finds a good thing, and it didn't stop there it goes on to tell who it is that favors him, it is the Lord that grants that favor.

To make it appear that the Lord doesn't know what He is saying, the Devil interferes with every marriage that takes place in this life. He wants them to turn out to be a sham so that he would benefit and the spiritually significant would be marred.

We must admit, the Devil knows some things we don't know yet. That is why he attempts to conceal the things that has heavenly ramifications, he can ill afford to watch us bathe in such revelation knowledge.

I am persuaded that two people living in the same house in harmony is a reflection of heavenly unity, peace and happiness. Once one catches that impression, that person would be hard to handle and the Devil knows it but hopes we never find out.

I know from personal experience that marriage is beautiful, I have been happily married to the same gracious woman for the past 43 years. She has been a genuine companion, one that is easy to live with and love. However, I know that my Lord has a place prepared for me that would surpass even my blissful marriage of many years. The place the Lord has will never end.

- **"Whoso findeth a wife findeth a good thing, and obtaineth favour of the LORD." (Prov 18:22 KJV)**

If married people would catch a glimpse of the significance of marriage, they would fight to the bitter finish to keep the devil out of their relationship. They wouldn't give up so easily and commence to seek new partners. They would, first of all, seek the Lord's gift and once they were drawn to the one that the Lord approved, they would strive to live happily there after.

Satan only needs a small opening to enter a marriage, and he could care less which party provides the crack, he just wants in. It takes one with a healthy spiritual life to recognize the enemy's approach. The moment a spiritually minded person senses that the ongoing situation is influenced by the Devil; he or she would take measures to bring the problem under the Holy Spirit's control.

To have an intimate relationship with another person opens the door for a clearer understanding of the meaning of the word relationship. Relationship is very important to the Master. According to the teachings of Jesus, it exceeds the performance of miracle and mighty works.

Jesus reiterated this fact when He asked Peter did he love Him. He is not just seeking servants, He wants a relationship, He wants a person to really know Him and serve Him for who He is and not just for what He can do.

When we do marriage right, we demonstrate God's mindset for relationships. This wonderful God given institution represents two minds in one place working together without conflict.

I am sure the Devil knows this. That is why he works so diligent to usher in confusion, he wants to blur the picture that God has put before our very eyes. He wants to sell the idea that marriage is a war zone where only a select few shall survive.

It is a little wonder the Holy Spirit inspired the Apostle Paul to speak as he did on marriage; he likened it to Christ and His church.

- "That he might sanctify and cleanse it with the washing of water by the word,
- 27 That he might present it to himself a glorious church, not having spot, or wrinkle, or any such thing; but that it should be holy and without blemish.
- 28 So ought men to love their wives as their own bodies. He that loveth his wife loveth himself.
- 29 For no man ever yet hated his own flesh; but nourisheth and cherisheth it, even as the Lord the church:
- 30 For we are members of his body, of his flesh, and of his bones." (Eph 5:26-30 KJV)

When a marriage conforms to the divine order it is both beautiful and revelatory. It gives us somewhat of a glimpse of what God has purposed for His church in the end. Just as a God ordained that marriage is built on love and relationship, so is a consistent walk with the Lord. It takes one's love for the Master to inspire him or her to pursue a consistent relationship.

Our Lord chose to investigate the man that He would grant the keys to the kingdom. The thing He wanted to know had to deal with Peter's love. The Lord knew that it would be useless to expect a relationship out of a person that didn't have the basics ingredient which is love.

- "So when they had dined, Jesus saith to Simon Peter, Simon, son of Jonas, lovest thou me more than these? He saith unto him, Yea, Lord; thou knowest that I love thee. He saith unto him, Feed my lambs.
- 16 He saith to him again the second time, Simon, son of Jonas, lovest thou me? He saith unto him, Yea, Lord;

> thou knowest that I love thee. He saith unto him, Feed
> my sheep.
>
> - 17 He saith unto him the third time, Simon, son of
>   Jonas, lovest thou me? Peter was grieved because he said
>   unto him the third time, Lovest thou me? And he said
>   unto him, Lord, thou knowest all things; thou knowest
>   that I love thee. Jesus saith unto him, Feed my sheep."
>   (John 21:15-17 KJV)

It is certain that Jesus was not campaigning to recruit more workers, He was looking for someone to feed His sheep, He knew that the absence of love would turn the feeder into a bleeder of the sheep and that would destroy all possibilities of a relationship.

You can add this to your memory bank, when a person's relationship with the Lord is lacking, that person has a very difficult time doing what he or she should toward others. . That is why so called Christian marriages are much like the non Christian's, we are trying to carry on an operation that God intended to be both spiritual and natural. We are trying to make them work just from the carnal side.

Many don't seem to know that marriage is spiritual as well as natural. It should first be spiritual. Secondly naturally, both aspects are important to make it work in the way God intended it to work.

It is a fact that any form of infraction could interfere with the harmony of a marital relationship just as any blunder could lead to spiritual distraction. This holds true due to the spiritual nature of marriage. It is somewhat like salvation, it must be according to the word else it falls into formalism.

You know what happens when one has part truth or acts on part truth, if a thing is partly true, you could be sure that it would be a whole lie. Satan is the author of part truth because he knows exactly what part truth would do for a person's future. It would leave that person spiritually bankrupt.

I would like to say here before I move on to something else, when two people enter a relationship but fail to carry it out according to the divine order, you can be sure the enemy will do his part to turn that relationship into a sham.

The Devil would enter in and seek to make marriage seem like it is too difficult to continue with that same person. The enemy would have a person believe that if he or she would change mates, life would be much happier and more complete.

The thought of switching mates is the mentality that opens the door for legalized adultery. When a person departs from his or her original partner without scriptural grounds and marries another that person would then be living in adultery.

Living in adultery is different from a person drinking liquor and then repenting and confessing his or her error. After repenting confessing and forsaking, that person is ready to move on, but when a person illegally marries a person, he or she makes his or her home in adultery, that would be more than a mistake, that would be a lifestyle. It is impossible to die in the Lord while living in adultery.

Just in case one of My Dear readers should be made to feel that I think that adultery is the only major sin, that is not what I think. I think that it is one of the more popular and convenient ones, it is one that is generally accepted by our spiritually blind society. However, the Lord has the last say and that just happens to be one of the subjects that He has much to say.

Let's face it, we have catered to the flesh so often and so long that we have allowed ourselves to almost forget that we must surely die. I don't think that dying is the problem, I think the way we choose to live is the thing that complicates the matter.

The fact that He compares it with His church that He shed His blood to purchase it; we should know that He wants the institution carried out in line with His word.

- "Take heed therefore unto yourselves, and to all the flock, over the which the Holy Ghost hath made you overseers, to feed the church of God, which he hath purchased with his own blood." (Acts 20:28 KJV)
- "That he might present it to himself a glorious church, not having spot, or wrinkle, or any such thing; but that it should be holy and without blemish." (Eph 5:27 KJV)
- Let us be glad and rejoice, and give honour to him: for the marriage of the Lamb is come, and his wife hath made herself ready.
- 8 And to her was granted that she should be arrayed in fine linen, clean and white: for the fine linen is the righteousness of saints.
- 9 And he saith unto me, Write, Blessed are they which are called unto the marriage supper of the Lamb. And he saith unto me, These are the true sayings of God." (Rev 19:7-9 KJV)

There is no way the Lord would write so much about marriage if it wasn't for the fact that He wanted us to see it as a natural thing with spiritual ramifications.

For the sake of the record, this chapter was added to remind us that even a good thing could interfere with a person's preparation for dying.

This

A Sober Look at the Reality of Death

A *ccording to the word of* God, every living person has an appointment with death. The way we live is the way we die and the way we die is the way we get up. If we live wrong, we run the risk of dying wrong. If we should die wrong, no amount of a flowers, nice words, or accolades are going to change how we have lived or change our reward after death.

It is high time that we take a sober look at how we live from day to day and ask ourselves, "Would I like to leave this life the way I am right now?" If the answer comes back absolutely not, we must then put forth our best effort to change what we know needs changing and prepare to meet our God.

If we would strive to be right with God with the same energy we employ to have fun, we would no doubt be ready when our hour arrived. We can't afford to cast the thought of death behind us and act as if it only happens to others. We must keep fresh in our minds that our day is sure to come, we just don't know when. However, the when of death is not as important as the how. The how of death deals with the question how will death find me, what lifestyle will I be living? God is well qualified to handle the when, it is my lawful duty to deal with the how, and I am given the responsibility to make my calling and election sure.

Every believer should know by now that our bodies have no desire for heaven. Human flesh is too satisfied with what's going on here in this life to even think of any other place. Everything the flesh knows, enjoys, expects or desires is right here on earth. The other life or the other world was designed for our born again spirits. That is why we must strive to maintain a good relationship with the Lord to keep our spirits strong enough to overcome the flesh.

The Apostle Paul addressed the church about this internal war that was going on between the flesh and the spirit. If we expect to die in the Lord, our spirits must dominate over the flesh, if our flesh wins out, we would disqualify ourselves for a happy ending.

- **"This I say then, Walk in the Spirit, and ye shall not fulfil the lust of the flesh.**
- **17 For the flesh lusteth against the Spirit, and the Spirit against the flesh: and these are contrary the one to the other: so that ye cannot do the things that ye would."** **(Gal 5:16-17 KJV)**

I pray to God that it won't take an eternity to reveal to us that much of what we concern ourselves with doesn't ever matter. Especially the things that perish with this world, the things that matter most are those things that have eternal value, mainly the soul.

Here on earth there are many things we strive to obtain. There are people living on this same planet and oftentimes in the same community that we live in, that don't have a trace of what we have, but are yet making out and tend to be happy with what they have. We strive to get more to go with what we have but the sad part is, it is done at the expense of our eternal soul.

The so called success criterion has duped us into believing that we should spend much more time gathering wealth and fame than we do seeking the face of God. Such mind-set has made us earthly rich and heavenly questionable. That is why we would rather discuss a variety of other subjects rather than death. It is not because we are unaware that we must die. We just hate to think about leaving all that we have accumulated here on earth. Our deepest worry should be that we have spent too much time preparing for here to qualify for the hereafter.

The feeling that the Apostle had, we don't seem to have when it comes to death. He called dying gain, we have been influenced to use the word loss when we speak of death but the word of God calls it gain, **"For to me to live is Christ, and to die is gain." (Phil 1:21 KJV)**

The man of God saw living longer would benefit the kingdom because he could and would preach longer. However, to die, he would gain what he had worked for. Death to him would be a blessing. He would join the ranks of the saints that have been counted worthy to escape the wrath to come.

When we view death from the scriptural standpoint, we see a tremendous difference between what it teaches, and what we seem to believe. We tend to feel that death takes away from us, but the Bible teaches what death gives us. The themes of death's rewards are in both Testaments.

Death takes us from the evil to come and places us in a place of rest, a place where our righteousness really pays off.

I strongly believe that the Lord calls some people home in the prime of life because of what He sees awaiting them in the future. He want the to avoid the enemies trap. He wants them while they are ripe and ready. Another year or two they might have drifted away from Him, so He calls them at His appointed time. We might be guessing but the Lord knows what's best for His children.

- **"The righteous perisheth, and no man layeth it to heart: and merciful men are taken away, none considering that the righteous is taken away from the evil to come.**
- **2 He shall enter into peace: they shall rest in their beds, each one walking in his uprightness." (Isa 57:1-2 KJV)**

When we choose to live godly and holy lives we are not really appreciated here on earth. When a godly person is removed, ones that have left an impeccable example, the sinful don't seem to pay enough attention to enquire as how living right is done or don't even raise the question as to how one could give up so much just to please God.

I may add that the premature death of a saint is much better than a record breaking life of a sinner, because those that have all on this side will miss it all on the other side. So then living a long sinful life has no advantage after death, it just gives one plenty time to get right with God before his or her departure.

- **"Though a sinner do evil an hundred times, and his days be prolonged, yet surely I know that it shall be well with them that fear God, which fear before him:" (Eccl 8:12 KJV)**

God's plan is by far the best design for the long haul because what it offers has no ending. The offers made here; end here, and their future is short lived.

God's plan for us is so complete that nothing could separate us from His wonderful love, not even death can keep us apart.

- "Who shall separate us from the love of Christ? shall tribulation, or distress, or persecution, or famine, or nakedness, or peril, or sword?
- 36 As it is written, For thy sake we are killed all the day long; we are accounted as sheep for the slaughter.
- 37 Nay, in all these things we are more than conquerors through him that loved us.
- 38 For I am persuaded, that neither death, nor life, nor angels, nor principalities, nor powers, nor things present, nor things to come,
- 39 Nor height, nor depth, nor any other creature, shall be able to separate us from the love of God, which is in Christ Jesus our Lord." (Rom 8:35-39 KJV)

The preceding text carries enough reason for any sober thinking person to want to connect with this unending love in this life knowing that it remains connected even after death.

Death to a believer could be looked upon as moving from a house of deterioration to one that never decays. Moving from a house that has too many leaks in the roof, broken windows, sagging floors, fading paint and uncomfortable dwelling death allowed us to move into our mansion.

- "For we know that if our earthly house of this tabernacle were dissolved, we have a building of God, an house not made with hands, eternal in the heavens." (2 Cor 5:1 KJV)
- We are taught to believe that this old house of clay the zenith of importance, we fail to realize that as long as we dwell in these earthly bodies we can only get so close

with the Lord, it is after this old house dissolves that we
would be home with Him.

- "Therefore we are always confident, knowing that,
whilst we are at home in the body, we are absent from
the Lord:" (2 Cor 5:6 KJV)

I would like to ask this question, which is better, to be here in this
world that hates you and the God you serve or to be with Him that love
you with no ending?

I think we have oversold this earthly life and undersold the life to
come. The Bible supports that the best is yet to come; we act as if the
best has already come.

- "For I am in a strait betwixt two, having a desire to
depart, and to be with Christ; which is far better:" (Phil
1:23 KJV)

When we consider the feeling that accompanies a truly spiritual
service, one where you wish you could continue to feel what you are
feeling. That is a sample of what being in the presence of the Lord
does for you. The thing that keeps it from being even greater, we are
yet dwelling in a physical body. The natural man can only take and
understand so much but imagine what it would be like if the body was
removed.

An anointed service serves as a reminder that we are much more
satisfied, complete, happier and at home in His presence than we are
anywhere else. The psalmist caught a glimpse of the difference that His
presence makes.

- **"Thou wilt shew me the path of life: in thy presence is fulness of joy; at thy right hand there are pleasures for evermore." (Ps 16:11 KJV)**

I would like to believe that one moment in the presence of the Lord would wipe away every memory of what we left behind. His presence would be so gratifying that we could only think of worshiping Him, for being so mindful of us and allowing us into His presence.

I repeat, we have undersold the value of a saint death and oversold long-life in this sin cursed world. However, the Bible gives us something to draw from to get us clear in our thinking.

- **"Precious in the sight of the LORD is the death of his saints." (Ps 116:15 KJV)**

You see what the Lord says about the death of His saints, He calls it precious or valuable which means means costly, as precious stones, dear, beloved, as relatives and friends, honored, respected, or splendid. Beautiful is how the Lord sees death when it is a saint.

- **"The idea here is, that the death of saints is an object of value; that God regards it as of importance; that it is connected with his great plans, and that there are great purposes to be accomplished by it. The idea here seems to be that the death of a good man is in itself of so much importance, and so connected with the glory of God and the accomplishment of his purposes, that he will not cause it to take place except in circumstances, at times, and in a manner, which will best secure those ends."**

(from Barnes' Notes, Electronic Database. Copyright (c) 1997 by Biblesoft)

Could it be that the lack of preaching and teaching on the subject of death has left us earthly intoxicated and heavenly blind? When we do speak of departing from this life our choice word is the rapture. We forget that some of us are going to die, that is the other transportation out of here.

The Bible does teach that some are going to be caught up to meet the Lord in the air, but it also teaches that some are going to fall asleep. Jesus made the word sleep popular after the death of Lazarus. When a saint dies, he or she is not really dead; he or she has just crossed over to the side of life that has no ending. It is called sleep because that person would have ceased from earthly activities.

Falling to sleep doesn't prevent one from being in the rapture; all we have to do is make sure that we are in the Lord.

- *"But I would not have you to be ignorant, brethren, concerning them which are asleep, that ye sorrow not, even as others which have no hope.*
- *14 For if we believe that Jesus died and rose again, even so them also which sleep in Jesus will God bring with him.*
- *15 For this we say unto you by the word of the Lord, that we which are alive and remain unto the coming of the Lord shall not prevent them which are asleep.*
- *16 For the Lord himself shall descend from heaven with a shout, with the voice of the archangel, and with the trump of God: and the dead in Christ shall rise first:*

- *17 Then we which are alive and remain shall be caught up together with them in the clouds, to meet the Lord in the air: and so shall we ever be with the Lord.*
- *18 Wherefore comfort one another with these words." (1 Thess 4:13-18 KJV)*

The words that we should use to comfort one another are the ones above. They are designed to correct our misguided thinking about death. We are to understand that death does not bring to an end the hope of eternal life. It means that we move from this earthly house to the one continues throughout eternity.

We should notice that being alive during the rapture doesn't give us an advantage over the ones that have already fallen asleep. We will all be caught up together to meet the Lord in the air. That should be a comforting thought to all, the fact that we are going back with Him if we fall asleep, or if we remain alive.

I am persuaded that there will be no discussion in heaven about how one got there. This question will not matter, "Did you die first or were you were alive when He called His church home?" We would be so glad to be there that how we got there wouldn't matter one iota.

I don't expect any discussion on one's condition prior to departing from this life. Were you're sick, did you drown, get run over by a train, in a plane crash, did you starve to death, where you in a fire, storm, flood, where you rich or poor, married or single, happy or sad? Being in the presence of the Lord would eradicate the need to answer the preceding questions and conditions.

Heaven will leave no grounds for bragging, boasting, weeping, sickness, disappointment or any of the things that mean so much to us down here.

I am often baffled at the way we preach funerals; the average preacher preaches most funerals as if the person was a saint. The preacher makes it almost impossible for the person to miss heaven, that is, according to their description of the deceased.

We love to leave the family feeling good about their loved one, but in reality, they know the person much better than the preacher would. They know when the preacher overstates the person's holiness. The family would quickly recognize when the preacher had the wrong description of the deceased and in the speaker's words he/she was attempting to send the person where they hadn't prepared to go.

Preaching a message at a funeral would provide a good opportunity to inform people about the Lord's word on death and what the Lord offers them that believe.

- **"Jesus said unto her, I am the resurrection, and the life: he that believeth in me, though he were dead, yet shall he live:**
- **26 And whosoever liveth and believeth in me shall never die. Believest thou this?"(John 11:25-26 KJV)**

Since we hear so little ministry on the subject of death, the majority don't have a clue on what the Bible actually teaches on the subject. If the average person that has heard anything on the subject of death, he or she heard it at a funeral. What was heard could have been exaggerated or diluted, it just depends on who they heard saying it.

Satan is known to enter wherever he finds an opening, he has influenced many preachers. Satan delights in seeing preachers openly lie over people that made little or no effort to go where the preacher was trying to send them.

I have said over the years, that I could preach a whole hour without calling the persons name or suggesting where the person was going. I know this, you can always tell where a person is going in the hereafter by what he/she go after here. Nothing changes after death. If the person pursued wickedness before his or her demise that person would have secured himself/herself a place in the lake of fire according to the word of God. Likewise, if a person lives a consistent holy life, that person would die in the Lord, his or her death would be precious in the sight of the Lord.

One thing for sure, the way we carry on after a person's death, we sure didn't get our method of operation from the Bible. We have no evidence in the Bible that the people made the kind of noise we make or showed the concern that we show. It appears that they just buried their dead and went on about their business. We even have an account that shows that the wife didn't even know that her husband was dead until the men arrived at pick her up for burial.

- **"But Peter said, Ananias, why hath Satan filled thine heart to lie to the Holy Ghost, and to keep back part of the price of the land?**
- **4 Whiles it remained, was it not thine own? and after it was sold, was it not in thine own power? why hast thou conceived this thing in thine heart? thou hast not lied unto men, but unto God.**
- **5 And Ananias hearing these words fell down, and gave up the ghost: and great fear came on all them that heard these things.**
- **6 And the young men arose, wound him up, and carried him out, and buried him.**

- 7 And it was about the space of three hours after, when his wife, not knowing what was done, came in.
- 8 And Peter answered unto her, Tell me whether ye sold the land for so much? And she said, Yea, for so much.
- 9 Then Peter said unto her, How is it that ye have agreed together to tempt the Spirit of the Lord? behold, the feet of them which have buried thy husband are at the door, and shall carry thee out.
- 10 Then fell she down straightway at his feet, and yielded up the ghost: and the young men came in, and found her dead, and, carrying her forth, buried her by her husband." (Acts 5:3-10 KJV)

We need to be constantly reminded in this life that we should be living to live again. We don't just need to live for what we can get in this life, because everything in this world is passing away. We shouldn't want to perish with this evil worlds' system operating in our lives. I am reminded of the song that says, "I don't want any trouble when I rise."

Fixed for Living with No Plans for Dying

*I*n this world, we are encouraged to make preparations for the future, but we basically mean the future in this world. We invest in life insurance, we spend endless hours trying to obtain more of the goods of this world, and we act as if we will be here forever.

The majority of our planning has to do with this life or better yet it has to do with life in this world. We tend to forget that we have a soul that must spend eternity somewhere. We fail to realize that it is in this life that we prepare for the life to come.

The earth has received many bodies that were counted a success while living in this present world. However, those same souls failed to realize that life went beyond this world. They were really fixed for living, but they had no exit strategy for dying. Their focus was on getting all that they could while dwelling on the earth. They failed to recognize that the day of death would surely come to all rich and poor alike.

The Lord left on record examples of the empty result of people that sought after all that they could get in this life while making to preparation for the life to come, I would like to highlight two such characters.

One of them was too selfishly engaged in doing what pleased him to pay attention to anyone else's needs. The window of opportunity was definitely opened to him, but he had no desire to enter until it was too late.

People that choose to live for themselves are so narrow in their vision of others, that it is easy for them to act as if they are the only ones on the planet. I have often said that the Lord doesn't give us more for us to have more; He gives us more so that we could do more to help others.

- **"There was a certain rich man, which was clothed in purple and fine linen, and fared sumptuously every day:**
- **20 And there was a certain beggar named Lazarus, which was laid at his gate, full of sores,**
- **21 And desiring to be fed with the crumbs which fell from the rich man's table: moreover the dogs came and licked his sores.**
- *22 And it came to pass, that the beggar died, and was carried by the angels into Abraham's bosom: the rich man also died, and was buried;*
- *23 And in hell he lift up his eyes, being in torments, and seeth Abraham afar off, and Lazarus in his bosom."* *(Luke 16:19-23 KJV)*

The man in the preceding text was rich enough to help many. Just in case he didn't choose to help multitudes, it was fixed that he wouldn't have very far to find someone that needed his help, **"which was laid at his gate."** The people that cared, placed the man that was in need at the gate of one that could help. The Bible points out that Lazarus also desired even as little as the crumbs from the man's table, but he got more attention from the dogs than he did the man that could help him.

Lord, help us to learn from this rich man. Help us to help others when we are in a position to do so. Please help us not shut up our bowels of compassion when someone needs our help. Help me Lord to forever remember that I must leave this world and help me not look down on anyone just because he or she is not blessed like me.

I learned from the text that the man knew who Lazarus was. He also had a good idea where he went after he died. That is why he, specifically names Lazarus and requested for him to aid him after he died.

- **"And he cried and said, Father Abraham, have mercy on me, and send Lazarus that he may dip the tip of his finger in water, and cool my tongue; for I am tormented in this flame." (Luke 16:24 KJV)**

The fact that he calls for Lazarus by name indicates that he felt that the beggar had it rough in the past world. However, now Lazarus had gone to a much better place than the place where he ended up. Now he is the one that needs help. evidently he felt that if anyone would help him, it would be Lazarus.

I am sure that if he could, he would have quickly changed places with Lazarus in the second life. It didn't take him long to realize that if he had it to do over that he would give up everything he had to avoid spending eternity in torment.

May the wisdom of God influence our hearts and minds to realize that the same thing could happen to anyone that is yet a resident of this earth? We could choose riches over readiness. We could be in a position to give help and withhold it and when we needed help it wouldn't be there. I think that the message to the Roman church is appropriate right here, **"For whatsoever things were written aforetime were written for our learning, that we through patience and comfort of the scriptures might have hope." (Rom 15:4 KJV)**

The Lord didn't put this revelatory message in the book just to make the book larger, it is there to instruct, inspire and direct us in the right way.

On this side, we can all see that the choice made by the rich man was a soul condemning mistake. We should do everything within our power to not make the same or a similar blunder.

When we revisit the life of the rich man we can see that he didn't seem to have been involved in the things we would consider *scandalous*. He didn't break up any homes, he didn't kill anyone, rob, drink or cheat on his wife; neither did he help where he could have. Regardless of what he didn't or did, he found himself in a permanent place one that is easy to enter but impossible to depart. May his fate send a strong message to every earth dweller, that nothing in this world is worth one losing his or her soul?

The saddest of it all what we go after here not only can't assist us, we can't take it with us or use it any more after we leave this life.

Lazarus died without having the riches of this life, but in the end he was rich enough to be sought out by one that had been rich most of his life.

The choice is clearly spelled out, if you get all that this world has to offer, you will miss out on what the world to come gives. However, it is in this life that we choose which we will have.

- **"See, I have set before thee this day life and good, and death and evil;"(Deut 30:15 KJV)**
- **"I call heaven and earth to record this day against you, that I have set before you life and death, blessing and**

cursing: therefore choose life, that both thou and thy
seed may live:

- **20 That thou mayest love the LORD thy God, and that thou mayest obey his voice, and that thou mayest cleave unto him: for he is thy life, and the length of thy days: that thou mayest dwell in the land which the LORD sware unto thy fathers, to Abraham, to Isaac, and to Jacob, to give them." (Deut 30:19-20 KJV)**

Just as ancient Israel had to choose between serving the true and living God or serving the gods that the nations served, we too must choose between being rich in faith or rich with what this world offers.

Israel couldn't take for granted that the land was theirs, they had to trust and obey the voice of the Lord.

Now let us take a look at another man that was very successful in this world but in the end, he was counted a fool. The man was so successful that he didn't have time for his most important reason for living. He was willing to put his soul on hold until he could accumulate more of what this world offer and then seek help for his soul.

In the introduction of this lesson Jesus made known that a man's life was not made up of the things that he possessed.

- **"And he said unto them, Take heed, and beware of covetousness: for a man's life consisteth not in the abundance of the things which he possesseth." (Luke 12:15 KJV)**

This most sober and saintly message has been ignored many times over. The record will show that everyone that took this warning lightly ended up spiritually bankrupt.

Achan lost his life and the life of his family because he failed to deal with the spirit of covetousness. He was like many, he felt that he had to get what he wanted while the door was open.

- **"When I saw among the spoils a goodly Babylonish garment, and two hundred shekels of silver, and a wedge of gold of fifty shekels weight, then I coveted them, and took them; and, behold, they are hid in the earth in the midst of my tent, and the silver under it." (Josh 7:21 KJV)**

Satan has been very successful in promoting the spirit of covetousness. He has been able to get us to shift our focus from things with eternal value to things that are passing away.

The enemy no doubt took great delight when the pulpits got carried away with the prosperity message as it was preached by many. They would have us believe that the Lord wanted all of His children rich and prosperous. The pulpit almost aborted the teachings that would have made a difference in how one should live and how one should prepare for death, so that everyone could prepare to stay here.

- **"If any man teach otherwise, and consent not to wholesome words, even the words of our Lord Jesus Christ, and to the doctrine which is according to godliness;**
- **4 He is proud, knowing nothing, but doting about questions and strifes of words, whereof cometh envy, strife, railings, evil surmisings,**

- **5 Perverse disputings of men of corrupt minds, and destitute of the truth, supposing that gain is godliness: from such withdraw thyself.**
- **6 But godliness with contentment is great gain.**
- **7 For we brought nothing into this world, and it is certain we can carry nothing out.**
- **8 And having food and raiment let us be therewith content." (1 Tim 6:3-8 KJV)**

The Apostle Paul would have been barred from speaking at our conferences, conventions, fellowships and local assemblies because he wants us to be content with just having food and raiment. We would say, he wants us poor like the majority, but we deserve God's best. The truth is he wanted us to focus on what matters the most and not to let fleeting things take us down lower than we need to go.

Notice the word of this spiritual man of God, **"supposing that gain is godliness: from such withdraw thyself."** We have heard many that were under that persuasion, they made it sound as if the more one had of this world, the greater his or her faith stood out.

The Apostle seemed to have thought that contentment was the badge of identification of one's progress spiritually **"And having food and raiment let us be therewith content."**

One of the things the enemy hopes never happens is that we should be happy doing the right thing. He wants us to always have something to complain about, that way he could keep us seeking something outside the Lord. When we are not satisfied with the things of the Lord, the enemy would import from a distant land anything we thought we had to have. He would make sure it would be according to our lust just to keep us from focusing on the Master.

A person that is content would rarely seek after things that are off limits. Neither would a person that is pleased with his or her relationship with the Lord seeks after things that will take him/her away from the Lord.

Jesus had something to say on the subject of priorities, He told us not to place perishable things above eternal things, that should be a message to all believers and for all times.

It is a fact that the church loses more people to covetousness, greed, lust and worldly ambitions than to any other sources. We are easy prey for the things of this world, we act as if we are here to stay and the more you have, the longer you could stay and the happier you would be. I think we should know by now that such thinking is untrue and unreal. It is best to lay up our treasures where they are protected by God's divine plan.

Jesus taught that one's crave for treasures indicated the place of the heart, in other words, one is known to pursue that which his or her heart desires the most.

- **20 But lay up for yourselves treasures in heaven, where neither moth nor rust doth corrupt, and where thieves do not break through nor steal:**
- **21 For where your treasure is, there will your heart be also." (Matt 6:19-21 KJV)**

After viewing the Bible characters as well as having lived long enough to have seen multitudes of people from every walk of life depart from this world by way of death, we know that nothing we accumulate in this life follows us into eternity. It is all left behind for the living

The successful, the rich and the poor alike are placed in the earth. They can no longer claim what's theirs in this world. It is all left for the use of someone else. The dead is finished with the world and all of its benefits.

The rich fool fell into the trap that many have fallen into and many more are sure to duplicate.

- **"And he spake a parable unto them, saying, The ground of a certain rich man brought forth plentifully:**
- **17 And he thought within himself, saying, What shall I do, because I have no room where to bestow my fruits?**
- **18 And he said, This will I do: I will pull down my barns, and build greater; and there will I bestow all my fruits and my goods.**
- **19 And I will say to my soul, Soul, thou hast much goods laid up for many years; take thine ease, eat, drink, and be merry.**
- **20 But God said unto him, Thou fool, this night thy soul shall be required of thee: then whose shall those things be, which thou hast provided?**
- **21 So is he that layeth up treasure for himself, and is not rich toward God." (Luke 12:16-21 KJV)**

The man in the preceding text is more than a rich fool. He is a rich pattern for all that are wise enough to realize that over-involvement and so called progress and success could lead to life's greatest loss.

To die having been rich in the natural world has no advantages in the world to come. With that being true, it seems wise to settle that matter in this world and go after the things that hold eternal value.

The fact is, one must die and return to the dust from which he was taken. This teaching has been in the existence since the first man and no one has the power to change that fact.

- "In the sweat of thy face shalt thou eat bread, till thou return unto the ground; for out of it wast thou taken: for dust thou art, and unto dust shalt thou return." (Gen 3:19 KJV)

- "For we must needs die, and are as water spilt on the ground, which cannot be gathered up again; neither doth God respect any person: yet doth he devise means, that his banished be not expelled from him." (2 Sam 14:14 KJV)

- "Seeing his days are determined, the number of his months are with thee, thou hast appointed his bounds that he cannot pass;" (Job 14:5 KJV)

None of us may understand the reason for death or even where one goes after death. One thing we know for sure is that people do die. Each of us could make a long list of names that we have seen depart from this life. Death is an appointment that no man will miss. Ready or not, when death comes for a person it doesn't have time to argue with a person neither does death ask one are you ready. It just takes whomever is assigned to its hand.

- *"And as it is appointed unto men once to die, but after this the judgment:" (Heb 9:27 KJV)*

In life some of us are known for being late, but when death comes, we can be sure that we will be on time for that last appointment. Some appointments we take great pain in preparing for, but when it comes to death the majority has seemingly divorced the thought from their minds. They act as if not thinking about it would postpone its coming, but not so, death is in every living man's future.

- "For I know that thou wilt bring me to death, and to the house appointed for all living." (Job 30:23 KJV)
- "What man is he that liveth, and shall not see death? shall he deliver his soul from the hand of the grave? Selah." (Ps 89:48 KJV)
- All go unto one place; all are of the dust, and all turn to dust again." (Eccl 3:20 KJV)

The fact that all living must die is taught in the scriptures. However, the pulpits have left us in the dark on that subject. What we know about death is basically what we hear discussed, much of it comes from opinions and not the Bible.

The Bible just informs us that it is coming. It doesn't go into detail, because death is not the problem. It is the condition that our lives are in when death arrives that would cause the problem.

It stands to reason that as long as death lasts, it would be wise if we would spend more time preparing for its arrival. However, just the opposite seems true. We put forth our hard work to stay on this side. In fact, we are willing to go to great lengths to improve our chances to remaining in this world.

In our ignorance, we make such statements as "I've never been on the other side, I know what's here." We may not know what's on the other side, but we should know one thing and that is, we must all die. I have heard it said upon the demise of a person that has suffered for a long period of time, they are better off now; they don't have to suffer anymore. The truth of that matter rests in the spiritual condition of the person.

If he or she didn't die in the Lord, his or her suffering, that is lifelong suffering would just be starting. Death is not a spiritual sanctifier, it just puts one in a position to commence to reap the benefits that he or she has sown. In other words, we cannot have peace if we have not sown peace. We cannot rise holy if we did not live holy. We cannot get up saved if we went down lost.

We cannot wait for death before we decide to be spiritual. Neither can we depend on someone else getting us to glory, that decision must be made by the individual, and it must be made in this life.

"For the living know that they shall die: but the dead know not any thing, neither have they any more a reward; for the memory of them is forgotten." (Eccl 9:5 KJV)

The truth is, nothing in this present world could stop us from dying, not fame, fortune, popularity, good health, talent or importance to others. We must die and whatever we possessed will be left for someone else. After we have been deposited by into the earth, we will soon be forgotten by the majority. What we felt that we had to do will be carried on by someone else; that's the way it is and there's nothing we can do about it. However, there is something we do, we can become more focused on how we are living daily and seek to eliminate every soul-hindering action and thought from our lives in this world.

- **"Whatsoever thy hand findeth to do, do it with thy might; for there is no work, nor device, nor knowledge, nor wisdom, in the grave, whither thou goest." (Eccl 9:10 KJV)**
- **"Then shall the dust return to the earth as it was: and the spirit shall return unto God who gave it." (Eccl 12:7 KJV)**

The fact is, our bodies are going back to the dust and our spirits are returning to the Lord. We should focus on supporting our spirits much more than we do our flesh. Because once it returns to its home, it would know nothing else, but our spirits must account for all we have done or not done while dwelling on the earth. Let me say to myself, and you read what I said to me, I cannot afford to allow my body to put my soul so deep in debt that it would take all eternity to pay. I must learn to live by the Jesus rule, "**Then said Jesus unto his disciples, If any man will come after me, let him deny himself, and take up his cross, and follow me.**"(Matt 16:24 KJV)

It is much better to deny the flesh of things it shouldn't have here, than to be denied His presence later.

Long Life or Right Living; (Think About It)

It is a good chance that you, My Dear Reader, have lived long enough to have seen people of all ages die. Some you felt were too young, too successful, too soon etc. We can tell from observation that death follows no certain human pattern. It doesn't consult with us before taking a person. Death picks up whosoever is on its list for that day and hour.

The truth of the matter is the reason we come to such a conclusion. We have in our minds that death comes by age or to people that are not important to us. We are wrong, death comes to us all maybe not at the same time, but it is sure to come. It would serve us better if we would think of death as God's business. Preparing for death would be our business. The Lord doesn't need help in carrying out His responsibility. We are the ones that need help because we fail to understand that we are pilgrims in this present world. This is not our permanent home, this is just the dressing room where we prepare for our real home.

Death does not discriminate. It might strike in a home that has only one child and takes that child in his or her senior year in college or high school or just after graduation. When this happens it seems unfair to the mother or father; however, it happens to someone all the time.

Some young lady marries her high school sweet-heart and fifteen months later she gives birth to a fine baby boy, then there years later her husband dies. To the human mind, that would seem so unfair but none of these things come without a reminder and warning. By the time we reach a certain age, every intelligent mind should know that none of us are here to stay.

Life has taught us that there is no certain pattern that death follows. Our safest practice would be to seek to be ready whenever it comes. We should not try to predict when it's coming, but just focus on preparing for its arrival.

We put much more emphasis on living longer than we do on living right. Living right puts us in line with the will of God, while living long is just another earthly benefit that could work for us or against us. If we would redeem the time, living long could make us a blessing to others and at the same time give us more time to make our calling and election sure. However, living long could give us more time to make blunders and yet miss out in the end.

People that can read and those that have a decent understanding are tremendously blessed. I say we are blessed because of the wealth of information that is available to us on so many subjects, including death. When we view death from the Bible standpoint, we see it as a necessary part of God's plan for mankind. We see that one man's sins ushered in death and one man's righteousness destroyed death for the believers. If you are a believer, Jesus has already dealt with death on your behalf. That is why right living is so important, it is much more important that the length of your life here on earth. If you live for the Lord, heaven is awaiting. I believe that one second in the presence of Jesus would compensate for everything you didn't have on earth and everything you suffered while living here below.

One of the things the gospel of salvation brings to us is holy instructions for living in this world. The Lord knows that flesh is subject to turn aside to the ways of this world . That is why He gives us His word to help us deal with the real enemy.

Let us not fix our minds on living long to the neglect of living right. It is yet wise to live each day as it was our last one. We should amplify the importance of holy and righteous living above long life.

May you find support for holy living in the following scriptures. I pray that they will minister to your mind, soul and spirit. May you take them to heart and put them to practice in your daily life.

I trust that every reader would appreciate that God gives us His word to aid us in living an acceptable life in this present world. The Lord didn't give us His wonderful salvation to leave us like He found us. He intended that we should be transformed into His likeness.

- **"For the grace of God that bringeth salvation hath appeared to all men,**
- **12 Teaching us that, denying ungodliness and worldly lusts, we should live soberly, righteously, and godly, in this present world;**
- **13 Looking for that blessed hope, and the glorious appearing of the great God and our Saviour Jesus Christ;**
- **14 Who gave himself for us, that he might redeem us from all iniquity, and purify unto himself a peculiar people, zealous of good works." (Titus 2:11-14 KJV)**
- **"Therefore we are buried with him by baptism into death: that like as Christ was raised up from the dead**

by the glory of the Father, even so we also should walk in newness of life.

- 5 For if we have been planted together in the likeness of his death, we shall be also in the likeness of his resurrection:

- 6 Knowing this, that our old man is crucified with him, that the body of sin might be destroyed, that henceforth we should not serve sin." (Rom 6:4-6 KJV)

- "For if ye live after the flesh, ye shall die: but if ye through the Spirit do mortify the deeds of the body, ye shall live." (Rom 8:13 KJV)

- "The night is far spent, the day is at hand: let us therefore cast off the works of darkness, and let us put on the armour of light.

- 13 Let us walk honestly, as in the day; not in rioting and drunkenness, not in chambering and wantonness, not in strife and envying.

- 14 But put ye on the Lord Jesus Christ, and make not provision for the flesh, to fulfil the lusts thereof." (Rom 13:12-14 KJV)

- "Know ye not that the unrighteous shall not inherit the kingdom of God? Be not deceived: neither fornicators, nor idolaters, nor adulterers, nor effeminate, nor abusers of themselves with mankind,

- 10 Nor thieves, nor covetous, nor drunkards, nor revilers, nor extortioners, shall inherit the kingdom of God.

- 11 And such were some of you: but ye are washed, but ye are sanctified, but ye are justified in the name of the

Lord Jesus, and by the Spirit of our God." (1 Cor 6:9-11 KJV)

- "Having therefore these promises, dearly beloved, let us cleanse ourselves from all filthiness of the flesh and spirit, perfecting holiness in the fear of God."(2 Cor 7:1 KJV)

- "And they that are Christ's have crucified the flesh with the affections and lusts." (Gal 5:24 KJV)

- "According as he hath chosen us in him before the foundation of the world, that we should be holy and without blame before him in love:" (Eph 1:4 KJV)

- "That ye put off concerning the former conversation the old man, which is corrupt according to the deceitful lusts;

- 23 And be renewed in the spirit of your mind;

- 24 And that ye put on the new man, which after God is created in righteousness and true holiness.

- 25 Wherefore putting away lying, speak every man truth with his neighbour: for we are members one of another." (Eph 4:22-25 KJV)

- "Dearly beloved, I beseech you as strangers and pilgrims, abstain from fleshly lusts, which war against the soul;

- 12 Having your conversation honest among the Gentiles: that, whereas they speak against you as evildoers, they may by your good works, which they shall behold, glorify God in the day of visitation." (1 Peter 2:11-12 KJV)

- "Love not the world, neither the things that are in the world. If any man love the world, the love of the Father is not in him.

- **16 For all that is in the world, the lust of the flesh, and the lust of the eyes, and the pride of life, is not of the Father, but is of the world.**
- **17 And the world passeth away, and the lust thereof: but he that doeth the will of God abideth for ever." (1 John 2:15-17 KJV)**

The preceding verses are being offered to strengthen your grip on right living. It is the only way to go to make life profitable in the end. The Lord knows that we need instructions on how to deal with rebellious bodies while living in this hostile world, all while trying to avoid a Devil's hell.

In reality, we should be so carried away with the fact that the Lord wants us to spend eternity with Him, that nothing else would matter. I am sure that our journey would be less difficult if our love and devotion to the Lord was where it belongs.

Three things we could be sure won't change; that is the flesh, the world and the devil. Our best defense against these enemies would be to love the Lord with our whole heart.

May we avoid being duped into believing that the Lord has changed His mind about what He wants out of us. He decided before the foundation of the world that we should be holy and according to the scriptures that is yet His plan?

Let us learn to focus on admonishing people to daily prepare to meet God and not leave them believing that they have many years based upon their age.

The rich fool felt that he had many years, that is why he pursued increase and neglected his soul. He didn't take under consideration that it wasn't for him to decide how long he had, the matter of when is God's call.

The sad thing about toiling, laboring, hustling and working at one's finger to the bone to accumulate things in this life, is when we die and leave it all. Being rich won't help in the hour of death and being poor won't hinder one from dying any more than being rich would help. Death is not impressed with what one has or doesn't have. When a person's number comes up, no doctor or medicine could spare that person on that day.

- "No one can hold back his spirit from departing; no one has the power to prevent his day of death, for there is no discharge from that obligation and that dark battle. Certainly a man's wickedness is not going to help him then.
- 9 I have thought deeply about all that goes on here in the world, where people have the power of injuring each other. I have seen wicked men buried, and as their friends returned from the cemetery, having forgotten all the dead man's evil deeds, these men were praised in the very city where they had committed their many crimes! How odd! 11 Because God does not punish sinners instantly, people feel it is safe to do wrong. 12 But though a man sins a hundred times and still lives, I know very well that those who fear God will be better off, 13 unlike the wicked, who will not live long, good lives-their days shall pass away as quickly as shadows because they don't fear God." (Eccl 8:8-13 TLB)

My Dear Readers, let us strive to live holy lives and not depend on someone standing over us to lie us into glory. It won't work because the

Lord has the books, and He knows how we have lived, He will not be sidetracked by what someone says that is contrary to His record.

It makes no real sense to lie for a dead person no more than it makes sense to lie to one, or lie on one. Lying won't help the deceased but lying will hurt the liar.

If you have doubts about a person but feel that you must say something, you should speak words that are true and don't try to change the way a person failed to live by lying.

I am sure you could find something good to say about the deceased, it would be safe to stay with that line of thought and stay away from bettering the person's spiritual status, that was the person's responsibility.

A Pre-Death Reviving: (The Need of the Hour)

*E*very child of God should focus on his or her daily need for reviving because none of us can afford to wait for the annual meeting bearing the title Revival. We can't wait for tomorrow's event when we are in need today. No one should know before us that the spirit man needs a refreshing touch. When we make that assessment, we should get busy seeking the Lord's help to bring to pass what we need the most.

We can't afford to wait until we feel that we are about to die to start making preparation, we need to make daily progress to advance our spiritual relationship.

The Psalmist had it right when he pleaded for recovery before his departure. None of us should want to depart from this life with a sub-spiritual life. we should want to know if it is well with our soul.

- "Hear my prayer, O LORD, and give ear unto my cry; hold not thy peace at my tears: for I am a stranger with thee, and a sojourner, as all my fathers were.

113

- **13 O spare me, that I may recover strength, before I go hence, and be no more." (Ps 39:12-13 KJV)**

Now when it comes to the thought of departing from this life, this prayer is a classic. It is one I think every believer needs to pray on this side and pray it often. "O spare me, that I may recover strength, before I go hence, and be no more." This person that has drifted from the safe place he or she has once known in the Lord, to an insecure place.

We shouldn't wait until someone else detects that we are not where we once were, that is our own responsibility to know and do something about it, as soon as we find out.

The request made by the Psalmist is to be spared until he can recover strength. In other words, he didn't want to die in weakness, and he wanted back what he had lost or allowed to drift or slide back. The word recover is a very interesting word; it says exactly what every living saint needs to have done.

- **Recover: to get back : regain, to bring back to normal position or condition; to make up for, to find or identify again; to save from loss and restore to usefulness: reclaim; to regain a normal position or condition" (Merriam-Webster Dictionary)**

The heart cry of every child of God should be to recover whatever has been lost before crossing over. We should never let ourselves rest contented when we know something is missing in our relationship.

It is a personal responsibility to make sure that the soul is ready for departure. We shouldn't want the soul to take off before checking to make sure that it has what is needed to have a safe flight?

It would take the person that had once been strong to detect weakness. We should never accept weakness, no matter what caused it, it is our duty to have it removed by recapturing our strength.

The request for the recovery of strength is an appeal for a personal revival, something every believer must have regularly or else he or she would surely drift back to his or her old ways. None of us can afford to die carrying out our old sinful habits. We need reclaiming, refreshing, restoring, awakening, and cheering up. We need to return to our original order of worshiping God.

The Psalmist did pray a senseless prayer, one that sought longevity. He only wanted to remain until he could recover, he didn't want to leave after having lost what was valuable. He wanted to recover all before his departure.

He didn't want to die with heavy clouds hanging over his head, he wanted to recover the joy and peace that he once knew. In other words, he didn't want to die with a long string of question marks hanging over his life.

That should be the attitude of every child of God, we shouldn't want to leave this earth with a dark shadow hovering over us and neither should we want to depart in a spiritual condition that reflects hopelessness nor spiritual death.

The cry for restoration should be a common call for one that has spiritual insight. He or she would know that the Lord alone could renew his or her spiritual status. To know that one's soul is in trouble, but maintain silence would be the epitome of irresponsibility.

The soul is the part of us that has divine connections. It will not sit silently by and pretend that all is well when it knows that trouble is ahead. The soul is known to cry out when conditions are not favorable to spiritual progress.

- "Why art thou cast down, O my soul? and why art thou disquieted in me? hope thou in God: for I shall yet praise him for the help of his countenance." (Ps 42:5 KJV)
- "Why art thou cast down, O my soul? and why art thou disquieted within me? hope thou in God: for I shall yet praise him, who is the health of my countenance, and my God." (Ps 42:11 KJV)
- "Why art thou cast down, O my soul? and why art thou disquieted within me? hope in God: for I shall yet praise him, who is the health of my countenance, and my God." (Ps 43:5 KJV)

I know that the preceding verses are synonymous, but they drive home the point to me. They teach me that the Lord wants us to get the message that one should listen to his or her soul when it is despondent. The soul detects things that the body readily ignores. The soul is in touch with the spiritual realm and knows when something is missing that should be active. When it feels a distance between it and its maker, the soul is sure to cry out or make noise to get our attention.

Whenever the soul is cast down you can be sure that it senses something that's out of order. It will not maintain silence in the face of neglect. It is sure to disturb or alert you or do something to get one's attention.

The soul came from God and has connections to Him. When it is near Him, It is most content, but if there is a breach between the soul and its creator, the soul could grow very disturbed. Its best moments are when it is in fellowship with the Lord.

When we allow the flesh to lead the way in life, we are sure to bring many hurts to the soul. Its origin is from heaven; therefore, it cannot feast satisfactorily on earthly things.

The thing that causes most of man's misery is his effort to satisfy himself with worldly things. His body may content itself with the goods of this life, but the soul will never find true satisfaction here below. It will not rest contented outside of divine fellowship. Joy in the soul is a necessary part of man's satisfaction. When sin deadens that joy, it would take a restoration to renew that joy. That is exactly what the Psalmist was feeling when he cried out to the Lord, **"Restore unto me the joy of thy salvation; and uphold me with thy free spirit." (Ps 51:12 KJV)**

He was not asking the Lord for salvation, he wanted Him to revive the joy that goes along with salvation. We should make the same request when we feel the loss of joy in our souls. We should cry out honestly for the return of the joy of the Lord, it is a necessary part of salvation.

No child of God should want death to overtake him or her after he or she has lost that soul-refreshing joy, peace-giving, soul-thrilling and heart-lifting joy.

Revival is God's answer to joylessness, coldness, apathy, indolence and spiritual indifference. When revival comes, life is restored, joy is renewed, hope rises to its highest level and the peace of God controls our daily lives.

Every child of God should want his or her soul revived on this side. We shouldn't wait until we cross over to seek renewal. We shouldn't want to depart from this life with thick clouds of doubt and fear hanging over our heads, and we should want the sunshine of His glory hovering over us.

We shouldn't pray, Oh Lord don't let me die, but rather don't let me die weak, cold, dry, indifferent, hypocritical, or lukewarm. Let me recover everything that goes with salvation before I back to the dust.

- **"Hear my prayer, O LORD, and give ear unto my cry; hold not thy peace at my tears: for I am a stranger with thee, and a sojourner, as all my fathers were.**
- **13 O spare me, that I may recover strength, before I go hence, and be no more." (Ps 39:12-13 KJV)**

The above prayer could be called a suitable prayer because it is fitting and proper for one that wants to regain the things that have been lost. Not ever prayer is proper or necessary, but this one definitely is because it has all the necessary qualities to make it proper.

Another thing that makes this prayer suitable, it is prayed in the place where changes could be made. It is not like the prayer that the rich man prayed, the rich man's prayer was prayed in hell and that is the wrong place to offer a helpful prayer.

- **"And he cried and said, Father Abraham, have mercy on me, and send Lazarus, that he may dip the tip of his finger in water, and cool my tongue; for I am tormented in this flame." (Luke 16:24 KJV)**

I would thank that hell is a terrible place to launch a prayer from, because all prayers prayed in hell will without a doubt go unanswered. It is my understandings that the residents of hell would all be praying. None are in a position to answer the cries of others.

The prayer for restoration is a prayer that should be prayed in this life. One needs to recover strength, vitality, hope, peace and joy on this side; this would cheer him or her up before moving on to the next life.

Revival is the only thing that could save a sinking soul from destruction, it is in this life that where revival is suitable for one's needs.

Revival is bringing change into the lives of those that were once bound, cold, indifferent, apathetic and far from God. Revival delivers us from coldness, apathy, indifference, slothfulness, worldliness and spiritual dryness. Revival restores our past relationship, freshness, joy and peace in the Lord.

Once a person has been close with the Lord, he or she cannot rest knowing that there is a breach between him and the Lord. He will not rest contented until that closeness is restored.

Since sin is the driver that takes us away from the Lord; repentance is the vehicle that brings us back. When God grants repentance, it is His way of saying come home.

That is the feeling that came upon the Prodigal son, and when he came to himself, home was the only satisfactory place for him. Not all sins instantly put us in the pig pen. Some thrill, deceive and bind us outside of the pig pen; nevertheless, all sin will drive us away from our father's house.

Sin is not to be toyed with under any circumstances because of its deadly consequences. Sin is a killer of the soul in the end and your joy in this present world.

Let us take a look at the word revive: to bring back to life consciousness, or activity: make or become fresh or strong again; to bring back into use.

Synonyms; recover, revive, rally, rebound, snap back, bounce back, get well, come to life, turn the corner, pick oneself up, pull one self together, snap out of it.

In short when one needs a spiritual awakening, any or all the above could take place and when it does, that person won't be the same after being revived.

Making sure that we are daily living in the spiritual sunshine of God's freshness and not in the wintertime of spiritual coldness should be taken personally.

I know that it is easier for the flesh to support coldness than it is to support the reviving of the soul. The flesh delights in the way of least resistance. The flesh has no appetite for denial.

When we stand before the Lord, the secrets of every life will be revealed. The things we did and the things we didn't do that should have been done will be noted.

Living Life to Miss Dying Twice

The Bible is our source of information that gives us the necessary instructions on how to prepare for death by living a saved and sanctified lifestyle. The Bible is a spiritual book written to direct lives into the spiritual realm. Man is spiritual as well as natural; therefore, he must have spiritual direction to get past natural inclinations that have been trained in the physical world. The Bible makes a marked distinction between that which is spiritual and that which is natural, carnal, worldly, earthly, sensual and earthly.

- **"Dearly beloved, I beseech you as strangers and pilgrims, abstain from fleshly lusts, which war against the soul;" (1 Peter 2:11 KJV)**
- **"And take heed to yourselves, lest at any time your hearts be overcharged with surfeiting, and drunkenness, and cares of this life, and so that day come upon you unawares." (Luke 21:34 KJV)**

- "For if ye live after the flesh, ye shall die: but if ye through the Spirit do mortify the deeds of the body, ye shall live." (Rom 8:13 KJV)
- "This I say then, Walk in the Spirit, and ye shall not fulfil the lust of the flesh.
- 17 For the flesh lusteth against the Spirit, and the Spirit against the flesh: and these are contrary the one to the other: so that ye cannot do the things that ye would.
- 18 But if ye be led of the Spirit, ye are not under the law.
- 19 Now the works of the flesh are manifest, which are these; Adultery, fornication, uncleanness, lasciviousness,
- 20 Idolatry, witchcraft, hatred, variance, emulations, wrath, strife, seditions, heresies,
- 21 Envyings, murders, drunkenness, revellings, and such like: of the which I tell you before, as I have also told you in time past, that they which do such things shall not inherit the kingdom of God." (Gal 5:16-21 KJV)

One of the first lessons to be learned is the fact that we are not what we appear to be. We may appear to belong here in this world, but on the inside we have other-world potential. God did for man something that He didn't do for other animals; He breathed into man the breath of life in order to make man a living soul.

Since we are a soul, we cannot cater to the flesh, the world or the devil and remain spiritual. We must walk in the light of the living word of God in order to survive in this life and prepare for the life to come.

Successful living consists of living holy in this unholy world while living in an unholy body, but giving necessary attention to one's holy soul.

The information and instructions Jesus gave His disciples are yet applicable to His followers today, **"Then said Jesus unto his disciples, If any man will come after me, let him deny himself, and take up his cross, and follow me." (Matt 16:24 KJV)**

Self-denial has always played a major role in the lives of the people that wanted to please the Lord. It is most important to train the flesh to serve the spirit and not allow the spirit to starve because the flesh is the main attraction. We must at all times maintain a consciousness that the world and the flesh work together, under the influence of the devil, to bring about our defeat.

The flesh loves what the world has to offer but the spirit cannot survive off worldly things. It would surely die if all it gets is that which is of this world. The spirit has eternal value, but the flesh returns to the dust. I sure wouldn't want my flesh to make such a large debt that it would take all eternity to pay.

Jesus said it best on the subject of gaining the world but in the end losing one's soul. That indeed would be a nonprofit lifestyle to get all this world has to offer, but in the end have none of what it takes to get to glory.

It is true that this world has much to offer the flesh and much of what it offers could be very gratifying to our lower nature, but it would surely disqualify the soul from entering into its happy home. In the end it wouldn't worth the whole world to lose one's soul.

- **"For what is a man profited, if he shall gain the whole world, and lose his own soul? or what shall a man give in exchange for his soul?" (Matt 16:26 KJV)**

According to the word of God, it is impossible to live after the ways of the world and yet maintain a good relationship with the Lord. Jesus taught His followers that one would have to lose his life in order to gain it in the life to come.

The strong challenge for living right in this wrong world is sure to come from within. These un-regenerated bodies are sure to maintain connection with the world. The human body is at home in this world. That is why we must kill our own flesh by denying it from participating in fleshly gratification that carries spiritual neglect.

- **"For anyone who keeps his life for himself shall lose it; and anyone who loses his life for me shall find it again." (Matt 16:25TLB)**

Satan takes the advantage of people who are overly moved by the things that this life has to offer. He is known to hoodwink people into believing that they are supposed to have more of every available thing this world has to offer. Those that think like that soon forget that death might show up at any moment. Many fail to realize that more of the world's things do not guarantee longer life. They forget that spending one's time catering to the flesh can lead to spiritual bankruptcy.

It was Jesus that warned His followers not to allow this life to intoxicate them and leave them blinded to the lateness of the hour. The cares of this life carry a strong influence. It is called trying to "keep up with the Joneses." Jesus called it the cares of this life.

- **"And take heed to yourselves, lest at any time your hearts be overcharged with surfeiting, and drunkenness, and cares of this life, and so that day come upon you unawares." (Luke 21:34 KJV)**

- "And these are they which are sown among thorns; such as hear the word,
- 19 And the cares of this world, and the deceitfulness of riches, and the lusts of other things entering in, choke the word, and it becometh unfruitful." (Mark 4:18-19 KJV)

The things of this life are known to lure one into a stupor and leave him/her aggressively pursuing things while forgetting the main thing. There is absolutely nothing we could accomplish in this world that would serve as a substitute for the loss of our soul.

The fact that the world has no substitute for the loss of one's soul, should give us all the more reason to forsake that portion of this life that would jeopardize our walk with the king.

Every believer should raise his or her sights to focus on the type of living that makes a lasting difference. We should strive for the lifestyle that carries eternal rewards.

God forbid that we should fall victim of the death craze that is sweeping the country. We put much more emphasis on dying than we do living. In our society, we can get more people to attend the average funeral than we can get to attend a regular worship service. Most edifices are large enough to accommodate the regular Sunday morning attendees. However, when one that is popular passes away, no ordinary building could accommodate the crowed that would attend.

It would be wonderful if we could get people to attend regular worship service with the same faithfulness that they attend funerals. They seem to forget that worship service is about Jesus, the one who died so that we wouldn't have to die twice. Worship service should be about how to prepare for death, not how to avoid it, but prepare for it since it is going to come to all.

Let me say in plain language death does not purify a person's life. The way one lives is the way he/she dies and the way one dies is the way he/she will be after death.

We have so sanctified death that it has turned people into liars when one dies. We make the most wicked- living people, saints when they die. We roll them into a place where many wouldn't go during their life time. The remarks given over them could leave one thinking that the deceased was spiritually changed through death. If their living has been as pure as their funeral service, they would no doubt end up in that city called Heaven.

There is a section on the average funeral program that calls for open remarks with a two minute limit per speaker, only God knows what might be said during that period. Many exceed the time limit, in the name of "making the family feel better."

People attend funerals that may not know the deceased, they just have a knack for attending funerals. Some attend to get a free meal during the repast. This concept was designed to feed the family and out of town guests. However, many with a buzzard-like spirit swoop in to stuff their stomachs and some even have the nerve to fix a plate to go. On some occasions, the food is low by the time the family returns from the grave site, because the funeral clean-up committee has indulged themselves and gone on their merry way until they hear about the next funeral.

It is to be regretted that we have made so little progress in our thinking when it comes to death and dying. We seem to think that death only visits other families and homes. We act as if our homes are off limits, and that we too are immune to death.

Every funeral we attend or hear about should send a reminder to our better judgment that it happens to us all. It should strike a chord in our hearts that I could be next. We should not put our heads in the sand and pretend that death just comes to certain people. Know this, it is sure to visit us all.

- **"The day one dies is better than the day he is born! 2 It is better to spend your time at funerals than at festivals. For you are going to die, and it is a good thing to think about it while there is still time. 3 Sorrow is better than laughter, for sadness has a refining influence on us. 4 Yes, a wise man thinks much of death, while the fool thinks only of having a good time now. " (Eccl 7:1-4 TLB)**

It is wise to live daily with dying in mind. When we do that we make much better decisions because we realize how quickly we could be removed from this life, and we wouldn't want to leave unprepared.

If we would read between the lines, we will find attitudes of the deceased from both sides. We would glean the thinking pattern of the wicked and the righteous.

According to the lesson that Jesus taught, there were two men, one was rich the other poor, yet they had one thing in common, they both died.

- **"And it came to pass, that the beggar died, and was carried by the angels into Abraham's bosom: the rich man also died, and was buried;**
- **23 And in hell he lift up his eyes, being in torments, and seeth Abraham afar off, and Lazarus in his bosom.**
- **24 And he cried and said, Father Abraham, have mercy on me, and send Lazarus, that he may dip the tip of his**

> **finger in water, and cool my tongue; for I am tormented in this flame." (Luke 16:22-24 KJV)**

After death both men ended up where they had reservations. The poor man was picked up by the angels and taken to a place of rest. He was not taken to a resting place just because he was poor; his lifestyle had followed the pattern that grants rest after death. "And it came to pass, that the beggar died, and was carried by the angels into Abraham's bosom:"

We hear no more from the poor man, no request, complaints, he was at rest or undisturbed by any troubles, appetites etc.

The end of these lives could serve as a notice to the living. They offer us insight on what to expect depending on the way we prepare.

I know that nothing is said concerning poor Lazarus' lifestyle. We know that he was not given rest just because he was poor. He evidently had made a reservation for a better place while he suffered here below.

It is my understanding that heaven is a prepared place for prepared people. You don't just enter that city just because you die. You must make your reservations while you are alive, Jesus is the only one who can approve your certification. He says the same to us as He said to Nicodemus, **"Marvel not that I said unto thee, Ye must be born again." (John 3:7 KJV)**

Dying without the new birth is a guarantee that you and the rich man and that failed to believe the plan of salvation, will have to spend eternity where there is no comfort.

The objective of every God- fearing soul should be to live life to avoid dying twice. The people that are born twice won't have to die but once. But those that are born just once will have to die twice. The second death is the one that every soul needs to flee. The reason we need to be absent is this death it puts you in the wrong company. It places you with those who hate the Lord.

To rescue man from the second death is the reason the Lord came to this earth. He suffered and died for our sins so that we could be born again. The new birth would remove us from the realm of the spiritually dead.

- **"And you hath he quickened, who were dead in trespasses and sins;" (Eph 2:1 KJV)**
- **"For the love of Christ constraineth us; because we thus judge, that if one died for all, then were all dead:**
- **15 And that he died for all, that they which live should not henceforth live unto themselves, but unto him which died for them, and rose again." (2 Cor 5:14-15 KJV)**
- **Jesus became our sin offering so that He could give us His righteousness and make us suitable to inherit eternal life.**
- **"For he hath made him to be sin for us, who knew no sin; that we might be made the righteousness of God in him." (2 Cor 5:21 KJV)**

According to the preceding verse, the Lord became what we were. We were victims of sin, He became sin for us or our sin offering. He became what we were so that He could make us what He is.

This is a very unequal exchange; He took what we had upon Him and gave us what He had in Him. We were sinners; He took our sins and gave us His righteousness. That exchange exceeds that of a man giving a billion dollars to a person for one penny. In this unequal exchange Jesus took our death and gave us His life.

Living a holy life keeps one in the spirit of Jesus' purpose for dying. He wanted to instill in us life and that more abundantly.

We could say, of a truth that no one wants us to avoid the second death more than Jesus. He has done His part, it is now up to us, we must overcome the things that seek to turn us aside.

- **15 And having spoiled principalities and powers, he made a shew of them openly, triumphing over them in it." (Col 2:13-15 KJV)**

I trust that the following information will aid you in your understanding of the second death and inspire you to be more than a conqueror. May the death of Jesus suffice on your behalf, that you would live life so that death would have to flee away.

- **"The Bible also speaks of "the second death" (Rev 2:11), which is eternal death, the everlasting separation of the lost from God in HELL. The "second death" is equated with "the lake of fire" (Rev 20:14), "the lake which burns with fire and brimstone...is the second death" (Rev 21:8).**
- **The apostle Paul speaks of death as an enemy, "The last enemy that will be destroyed is death" (1 Cor 15:26). In His resurrection, Jesus conquered death-physical, spiritual, and eternal. Through fear of death, men are subject to bondage (Heb 2:15); but "our Savior Jesus Christ...has abolished death and brought life and immortality to light through the gospel" (2 Tim 1:10)."**

- (from Nelson's Illustrated Bible Dictionary, Copyright (c)1986, Thomas Nelson Publishers)

- "[This is the second death] That is, this whole process here described-the condemnation, and the final death and ruin of those whose names are "not found written in the book of life" - properly constitutes the second death. This proves that when it is said that "death and hell were cast into the lake of fire," it cannot be meant that all punishment will cease forever, and that all will be saved, for the writer goes on to describe what he calls "the second death" as still existing. See Rev 20:15. John describes this as the second death, not because it in all respects resembles the first death, but because it has so many points of resemblance that it may be properly called "death." Death, in any form, is the penalty of law; it is attended with pain; it cuts off from hope, from friends, from enjoyment; it subjects him who dies to a much-dreaded condition, and in all these respects it was proper to call the final condition of the wicked "death" - though it would still be true that the soul would live. There is no evidence that John meant to affirm that the second death would imply an extinction of "existence." Death never does that; the word does not naturally and properly convey that idea." (Rev 20:14) (from Barnes' Notes, Electronic Database. Copyright (c) 1997 by Biblesoft)

Death by One, The Resurrection by the Other

- "For since by man came death, by man came also the resurrection of the dead." (1 Cor 15:21 KJV)

During the average discussion on the subject of death, the majority seems to agree that Adam opened the door for death with his disobedience. However, many of the conversations seem to overlook the fact that Jesus opened another door so that death would not be the end for mankind.

It should be soul-refreshing to realize that everything that Adam did to set us back, Jesus did something to open the door for our recovery. Just as Adam's disobedience ushered in death, Jesus' obedience brought in life beyond the grave.

We no longer need to dwell on Adam's transgression, which made us sinners; we can now concentrate on Jesus' obedience, which makes one righteous.

The Apostle Paul said it best when discussing that resurrection, **"If in this life only we have hope in Christ, we are of all men most miserable."** (1 Cor 15:19 KJV)

It is a fact that all died in Adam, but let us not overlook the fact that Jesus opened the door for life and that more abundantly. Through His obedience, He brought life back into existence through His resurrection from the dead.

The Apostle Peter calls it a living hope that was purchased by the resurrection of Jesus from among the dead.

- **"Blessed be the God and Father of our Lord Jesus Christ, which according to his abundant mercy hath begotten us again unto a lively hope by the resurrection of Jesus Christ from the dead,**
- **4 To an inheritance incorruptible, and undefiled, and that fadeth not away, reserved in heaven for you,**
- **5 Who are kept by the power of God through faith unto salvation ready to be revealed in the last time." (1 Peter 1:3-5 KJV)**

After Jesus arose from the dead, every promise He had made came alive and was made possible for everyone that believes. We could move from Adam's side of death to Jesus' side of life.

- **"For as in Adam all die, even so in Christ shall all be made alive." (1 Cor 15:22 KJV)**
- **Adam's transgression dealt a blow to the whole human race but Jesus' resurrection opened the door of life and hope for the human family.**
- **"For since by man came death, by man came also the resurrection of the dead." (1 Cor 15:21 KJV)**

Jesus allowed death to feed upon Him for three days and nights, then He arose triumphantly from the grave. When He arose from the dead, hope came alive. Now everyone that believes in Him becomes a candidate for the resurrection from the dead.

Let us not spend the rest of our days dwelling on the unpleasant position that Adam put us in. We should shift our focus on the eternal plan that is offered through faith in Jesus Christ.

- **"But our citizenship is in heaven. And we eagerly await a Savior from there, the Lord Jesus Christ, 21 who, by the power that enables him to bring everything under his control, will transform our lowly bodies so that they will be like his glorious body." (Phil 3:20-21**
- **(from NIV)**
- **"Behold, I shew you a mystery; We shall not all sleep, but we shall all be changed,**
- **52 In a moment, in the twinkling of an eye, at the last trump: for the trumpet shall sound, and the dead shall be raised incorruptible, and we shall be changed.**
- **53 For this corruptible must put on incorruption, and this mortal must put on immortality.**
- **"For if we believe that Jesus died and rose again, even so them also which sleep in Jesus will God bring with him.**
- **15 For this we say unto you by the word of the Lord, that we which are alive and remain unto the coming of the Lord shall not prevent them which are asleep.**
- **16 For the Lord himself shall descend from heaven with a shout, with the voice of the archangel, and with the trump of God: and the dead in Christ shall rise first:**

- 17 Then we which are alive and remain shall be caught up together with them in the clouds, to meet the Lord in the air: and so shall we ever be with the Lord.
- 18 Wherefore comfort one another with these words." (1 Thess 4:14-18 KJV)

It appears that the church as a whole has failed to comfort one another with the preceding words. We have failed to clearly present the hope side of death, and we talk about death coming, but little about where we go after death.

When we consider the garden before Adam sinned, it was without the daily problems we face today. It appeared to be a peaceful place where harmony ruled and fellowship prevailed. When sin entered that all changed, the door was opened for pain, sickness, fear and everything else we know today including death.

Jesus changed the name of death when His friend Lazarus died, He called it sleep. If a person is asleep, he or she should be able to wake up; but he or she is dead it wouldn't be possible to awaken such a one. So when the saint departs from this life believing in the finished work of Jesus, they would only be sleeping. The Lord would have no trouble waking them up because He is the resurrection and the life.

- "These things said he: and after that he saith unto them, Our friend Lazarus sleepeth; but I go, that I may awake him out of sleep.
- 12 Then said his disciples, Lord, if he sleep, he shall do well.
- 13 Howbeit Jesus spake of his death: but they thought that he had spoken of taking of rest in sleep.

- 14 Then said Jesus unto them plainly, Lazarus is dead."
(John 11:11-14 KJV)

The foundation of the Christian faith rests upon the resurrection. It is impossible for one to have healthy faith without accepting the fact that Jesus arose from the dead. It was the heart of the message that His followers preached, they offered a hopeless world hope through the resurrection.

- "Moreover, brethren, I declare unto you the gospel which I preached unto you, which also ye have received, and wherein ye stand;
- 2 By which also ye are saved, if ye keep in memory what I preached unto you, unless ye have believed in vain.
- 3 For I delivered unto you first of all that which I also received, how that Christ died for our sins according to the scriptures;
- 4 And that he was buried, and that he rose again the third day according to the scriptures:
- 5 And that he was seen of Cephas, then of the twelve:"
(1 Cor 15:1-5 KJV)

The disciples had witnessed the Lord's presence after the resurrection, and they heard what He said before He was put to death. They were there when Mary and Martha confronted Jesus about the loss of their brother. They heard Jesus explain that hope was not lost just because Lazarus had fallen to sleep. They witnessed Jesus raising Lazarus from the dead. They could reason that He did it once, He could do it again, and since He did it for Lazarus; He would do it for all that believe.

That is why they went everywhere preaching the resurrection; they were offering hope to the hopeless.

Just as the disciples saw Jesus raising Lazarus from the dead, it is a good chance, they saw the saints that came up out of the graves after His resurrection and went into the city, and were seen by many.

- **"And the graves were opened; and many bodies of the saints which slept arose,**
- **53 And came out of the graves after his resurrection, and went into the holy city, and appeared unto many." (Matt 27:52-53 KJV)**

Since the scripture didn't say that the disciples saw the saints that came out of the graves, I won't say that they did, but it stands to reason that they saw them or some of them, since they went into the city. Even if they didn't see them, I am sure they heard what had happened because people have always been known to talk about unusual occurrences and this was truly unusual.

The Holy Spirit left on record many supernatural activities to build our faith. The Lord wants us to benefit from His resurrection, if we believe He will raise us up after death.

He spoke this truth to Mary and that message holds true today for all that believe.

I offer the following scriptures for you to feed your faith on and may we develop an appetite for the Lord's presence that would raise us above the fear of death.

- **"Jesus saith unto her, Thy brother shall rise again.**
- **24 Martha saith unto him, I know that he shall rise again in the resurrection at the last day.**

- 25 Jesus said unto her, I am the resurrection, and the life: he that believeth in me, though he were dead, yet shall he live:
- 26 And whosoever liveth and believeth in me shall never die. Believest thou this?" (John 11:23-26 KJV)
- "And this is the Father's will which hath sent me, that of all which he hath given me I should lose nothing, but should raise it up again at the last day.
- 40 And this is the will of him that sent me, that every one which seeth the Son, and believeth on him, may have everlasting life: and I will raise him up at the last day." (John 6:39-40 KJV)
- "But if the Spirit of him that raised up Jesus from the dead dwell in you, he that raised up Christ from the dead shall also quicken your mortal bodies by his Spirit that dwelleth in you." (Rom 8:11 KJV)
- "But now is Christ risen from the dead, and become the firstfruits of them that slept.
- 21 For since by man came death, by man came also the resurrection of the dead.
- 22 For as in Adam all die, even so in Christ shall all be made alive.
- 23 But every man in his own order: Christ the firstfruits; afterward they that are Christ's at his coming.
- 24 Then cometh the end, when he shall have delivered up the kingdom to God, even the Father; when he shall have put down all rule and all authority and power.
- 25 For he must reign, till he hath put all enemies under his feet.

- 26 The last enemy that shall be destroyed is death." (1 Cor 15:20-26 KJV)
- "But the rest of the dead lived not again until the thousand years were finished. This is the first resurrection." (Rev 20:5 KJV)
- "And God shall wipe away all tears from their eyes; and there shall be no more death, neither sorrow, nor crying, neither shall there be any more pain: for the former things are passed away." (Rev 21:4 KJV)

The death burial and resurrection of Jesus greatly changed the outlook of death. When it is seen through the eyes of salvation; it would be a promotion to a child of God because it removes us from a troublesome land to one where trouble cannot enter.

When death is viewed from a Biblical standpoint, when death overtakes a believer, it would be a blessing for one to give up this life for a better and eternal one.

It would be like moving from a deteriorating house to one that is leak-proof, thief-protected, and fire-proofed; one that won't decay. This is a real deal, to leave this house of clay and move into one that has no ending.

- "For we know that if our earthly house of this tabernacle were dissolved, we have a building of God, an house not made with hands, eternal in the heavens.
- 2 For in this we groan, earnestly desiring to be clothed upon with our house which is from heaven:
- 3 If so be that being clothed we shall not be found naked.

- **4 For we that are in this tabernacle do groan, being burdened: not for that we would be unclothed, but clothed upon, that mortality might be swallowed up of life." (2 Cor 5:1-4 KJV)**

The Apostle Paul made death sound like a graduation for a believer. He welcomed it, since he had fought a good fight and finished his course. Death would position him to receive his degree for the work he had done or the race he had run and the faith he had remained faithful to. He didn't sound in any measure that death would be a plan-wrecker, it was rather a promotion.

- **"For I am now ready to be offered, and the time of my departure is at hand.**
- **7 I have fought a good fight, I have finished my course, I have kept the faith:**
- **8 Henceforth there is laid up for me a crown of righteousness, which the Lord, the righteous judge, shall give me at that day: and not to me only, but unto all them also that love his appearing." (2 Tim 4:6-8 KJV)**

It appears to me that the Bible believers welcomed death as much as we dread it. They saw death as a process to get to the Lord. Living in this life was an opportunity to serve Him, but dying was the way to follow Him home. I would like to add, I would think that going home with the Lord would be much better than remaining here on this troublesome earth.

The Holy Spirit made it plain that this promotion was not limited to the Apostle Paul, it extended to all that love His appearing.

The fact that it is for all that have qualified puts this teaching in line with other teachings that the Apostle had given. It is always a blessing when the teacher teaches that which he/she believes in and practices.

It is also a blessing when one knows that God's word is not limited to a certain group, it is a universal gospel. It is able to save anyone and everyone that puts his or her trust in the word.

- **"Those things, which ye have both learned, and received, and heard, and seen in me, do: and the God of peace shall be with you." (Phil 4:9 KJV)**

You notice the certainty in which the man of God writes, he sounds convinced that the one that would follow the things that he had taught, would have the Lord's presence to support him/her.

That is why the Apostle Paul could feel so confident that dying would be a blessing, he had practiced what he had preached. What he had taught and preached was in line with the will of God and according to the word of God, death cannot prevent the fulfillment of God's word.

- **"According to my earnest expectation and my hope, that in nothing I shall be ashamed, but that with all boldness, as always, so now also Christ shall be magnified in my body, whether it be by life, or by death.**
- **21 For to me to live is Christ, and to die is gain.**
- **22 But if I live in the flesh, this is the fruit of my labour: yet what I shall choose I wot not.**
- **23 For I am in a strait betwixt two, having a desire to depart, and to be with Christ; which is far better:" (Phil 1:20-23 KJV)**

- "For we know that the whole creation groaneth and travaileth in pain together until now.
- 23 And not only they, but ourselves also, which have the firstfruits of the Spirit, even we ourselves groan within ourselves, waiting for the adoption, to wit, the redemption of our body." (Rom 8:22-23 KJV)
- "Therefore we are always confident, knowing that, whilst we are at home in the body, we are absent from the Lord:" (2 Cor 5:6 KJV)

The thought of being absent from the Lord while living here in the body or in this world should serve an indication that as good as things may be now, our better days are ahead.

The attitude we take toward this world has great influence on the decisions we make for eternity. Now if we should cherish this world and the things that it offers to the neglect of our soul and a life in heaven; we would have treated this world as our final home. The saints of old considered themselves as pilgrims and strangers in this world. They realized that they were just passing through; this world was not their home.

- "Hear my prayer, O LORD, and give ear unto my cry; hold not thy peace at my tears: for I am a stranger with thee, and a sojourner, as all my fathers were." (Ps 39:12 KJV)
- "Dearly beloved, I beseech you as strangers and pilgrims, abstain from fleshly lusts, which war against the soul;" (1 Peter 2:11 KJV)
- "These all died in faith, not having received the promises, but having seen them afar off, and were persuaded of

them, and embraced them, and confessed that they were strangers and pilgrims on the earth." (Heb 11:13 KJV)
- "those who use the things of the world, as if not engrossed in them. For this world in its present form is passing away." (1 Cor 7:31(from NIV)

Since we know that this present world in its form will pass away, we should not get too engrossed in the activities of this life. We shouldn't want to go down with a sinking ship.

Jesus said it best in describing to His followers the present dangers that would hinder one's outlook for the future:

- "And take heed to yourselves, lest at any time your hearts be overcharged with surfeiting, and drunkenness, and cares of this life, and so that day come upon you unawares." (Luke 21:34 KJV)

Jesus knew that the world had much to offer the flesh. He warned His followers not to overly indulge in the things of this life. They would be at risk since they didn't know what hour their Lord would call.

Let us therefore, enjoy the things that won't jeopardize our relationship with the Lord and be thankful for things being as well as they are. It is time for us to look up because our redemption draws closer with the passing of each day.

OTHER BOOKS BY BISHOP CLIFTON JONES, THESE
BOOKS MAY BE ORDERED IN THE FOLLOWING WAYS:
CHECK OUT OUR WEB SITE: jtchurch.com
JERUSALEM TEMPLE CHURCH
414 IVY STREET
PHILADELPHIA, MS 39350
601-562-3703
601-259-2412
601-416-2632 CELL
E-MAIL: cliftonbcj@aol.com   FAX: 6O1-656-9645
Mayfrancesjones@aol.com

YOU MAY MAIL ORDER ANY OF OUR MATERIAL BY
WRITING US AT
JERUSALEM CHURCH 414 IVY STREET PHILADELPHIA,
MS. 39350
DON'T FORGET OUR WEB-SITE@ JTCHURCH.COM
PRAYER CLINIC MANUAL
FAITH CLINIC MANUAL
LORD HEAL ME FROM THE INSIDE
HOW TO KEEP THE DEVIL OUT OF YOUR BUSINESS
I THOUGHT IT WAS THE DEVIL BUT IT WAS ME TOO
FASTING AND PRAYER FOR CHANGE
IT'S ALL ABOUT LOVE
A LITTLE KINDLING FOR YOUR FIRE
YOU NEED TO GROW UP
TOUGH FAITH
SOBER ADVICE FOR LAST DAY LIVING
FALLING IN THE WRONG PLACES
DYING AT THE DOCTORS DOOR

Bishop Clifton Jones

MISTAKEN IDENTITY
ARE YOU INDICTING ME?
PRAYER CLINIC WORKBOOK
FAITH CLINIC WORKBOOK
RUT OR REVIVAL
UNDER ATTACK BUT EQUIPPED TO STAND
IS IT OLD FASHIONED OR SAFE SANCTIFICATION?
GOD'S MEDICINE FOR THE WHOLE FAMILY
HOW PREACHERS COMMIT SUCIDE
HOLINESS TEACHING IN UNHOLY TIMES
A REQUEST FOR DIVINE INSPECTION
RAPED IN THE PRESENCE OF WITNESSES

CPSIA information can be obtained
at www.ICGtesting.com
Printed in the USA
FSOW01n0657280116
16296FS